The Unseen World of Angels and Demons

By the same author:

A FORETASTE OF HEAVEN (Autobiography)
ALLAH OR THE GOD OF THE BIBLE –
    WHAT IS THE TRUTH?
BEHOLD HIS LOVE
FATHER OF COMFORT (Daily Readings)
HIDDEN IN HIS HANDS
IF I ONLY LOVE JESUS
IN OUR MIDST – JESUS LOVES AND SUFFERS TODAY
IN THE FATHER'S REFINING HAND
MORE PRECIOUS THAN GOLD
MY ALL FOR HIM
PATMOS – WHEN THE HEAVENS OPENED
PRAYING OUR WAY THROUGH LIFE
REALITIES – THE MIRACLES OF GOD EXPERIENCED TODAY
REPENTANCE – THE JOY-FILLED LIFE
RULED BY THE SPIRJT
THE BLESSINGS OF ILLNESS
THE CHRISTIAN'S VICTORY
THE EVE OF PERSECUTION
THE HIDDEN TREASURE IN SUFFERING
WHAT COMES AFTER DEATH?

The Unseen World of Angels and Demons

BASILEA SCHLINK

Published by
chosen books

FLEMING H. REVELL COMPANY
OLD TAPPAN, NEW JERSEY

Original title: *Reiche der Engel und Dämonen*
First German edition — 1972
First British edition — 1985

Library of Congress Cataloging-in-Publication Data
Schlink, Basilea.
    The unseen world of angels and demons.

    Translation of: Reiche der Engel und Dämonen.
    1. Angels. 2. Demonology. I. Title.
BT966.2.S3513   1986   235   86-12973
ISBN 0-8007-9086-3

Contents

Demons – A Reality

1
Satanic Power — What Is Its Origin?

The demonic world — never has its reality been so evident as in our times, and never has the question been so pertinent: Where does this evil force come from and what is its origin? A question touching the limits of our human understanding. The apostle Paul, for instance, speaks of the "mystery of iniquity" (2 Thessalonians 2:7 AV). From the beginnings of Church history, Church Fathers and believers inspired by the Holy Spirit have sought to define the allusions made in the Scriptures on this topic. With their expositions they lift slightly the veil of mystery surrounding the power of evil, allowing us a glimpse of its role in God's eternal purposes. Even if some of the statements on the following pages are mere suppositions, bordering on the legendary, behind them are deep divine truths.

Various passages in the books of the Prophets imply that the adversary of God and accuser of man, referred to in the Bible as Satan (Job 1:6ff.), used to be a bright and shining being, a magnificent angelic prince. According to Isaiah 14:12 and Ezekiel 28:12ff., it would appear that the "Day Star", the "anointed guardian cherub", the "son of the morning", was none other than Lucifer, whose name means the "light bearer". Presumably he was one of the mightiest, perhaps the first, of all the angels to be created and thus the eldest of the "sons of God", as the angels are also called.

The words of the prophet Ezekiel may well refer to him: "You were the perfection of wisdom and beauty. You were in Eden, the garden of God; your clothing was bejeweled with every precious stone — ruby, topaz, diamond, chrysolite, onyx, jasper, sapphire, carbuncle, and emerald — all in beautiful settings of finest gold. They were given to you on the day you were created. I appointed you to be the anointed guardian cherub. You had access to the holy mountain of God. You walked among the stones of fire. You were perfect in all you did from the day you were created until that time when wrong was found in you" (Ezekiel 28:12-15 LB).

The power and greatness of this "son of light" must have been beyond imagination. As the "light bearer" of God he would have manifested and reflected the divine glory and beauty in all their fullness. He would have been the pride and joy of God. And as the mightiest of all angels he would have been endowed with the greatest authority. In accordance with his profound knowledge of God and the fullness of divine life and ardour that Lucifer bore within him, he would have been entrusted with the greatest and most beautiful domain in God's creation. He would have held the highest throne of the angels and have taken his place in God's holy council.

The story of the fall of this powerful and magnificent personage, the rebellious "son of the morning", is told in Isaiah: "For you said to yourself, 'I will ascend to heaven and rule the angels [literally, "the stars of God"]. I will take the highest throne. I will preside on the Mount of Assembly far away in the north. I will climb to the highest heavens and be like the Most High'" (Isaiah 14:13f. LB). In Ezekiel we read on: "So I drove you in disgrace from the mount

10

of God, and I expelled you, O guardian cherub, from among the fiery stones. Your heart became proud on account of your beauty, and you corrupted your wisdom because of your splendor. So I threw you to the earth" (Ezekiel 28:16f. NIV).

Isaiah alludes to the hour when Lucifer's pride and ambition were manifested: "I will be like the Most High!" And that was Lucifer's undoing. The devil, says Jesus, "does not stand in the truth" (John 8:44 RAV), and the fallen angels "did not keep their proper domain, but left their own habitation", as Jude writes (v.6 RAV).

How did this fall happen? There is a legend that can help us to visualize that hour of trial when the first battle was fought between Lucifer and Michael:

"When God announced to the angels His intention to create man, whose dwelling-place would be the earth, Lucifer was faced with a new situation. God was going to create new beings, humans, who were to live on earth, Lucifer's domain. They were to be a new order of creation, made in the image of God and equal to the angels in the sight of God. This thought was unbearable to Lucifer, who wanted to be more than man and to lord it over him. Lucifer wanted to acknowledge man only as a subordinate, a vassal, subject to him alone and punishable by him alone.

"The Lord then put Lucifer in his place. 'One and all are created beings, and one and all are subject to the Maker. To man is granted the sonship of God.'

"At this word of the Lord, Lucifer's countenance darkened. God warned him, 'Your pride will be your undoing. Beware, lest death should enter the world!'

"But it was already too late. Lucifer replied, 'I shall fight against You and against death so as to win divine life for myself!' And, supported by his adher-

11

ents, he opposed the Son of God with all his might...

"God was silent. For the first time darkness fell upon the angels and all creation. In the testing that followed, each angel had to stand or fall on his own; none could see the other. God Himself was hidden from sight. The darkness thickened, the tension mounted. Lucifer cried out, 'I am who I am!' and at the sound of his voice his adherents were compelled to repeat the cry.

"God was still silent. Then from one of the angelic choirs came a voice, humble but firm: 'God is God! Who is like God!'

"Two camps formed. The decision was made — for God or against Him. Mighty forces struggled in silent combat. Enveloped in clouds of darkness, God pronounced these words over this scene of division: 'Henceforth there shall be conflict in creation between light and darkness, love and hatred, humility and pride. Who will fight against Lucifer?'"

A call that has echoed down through the ages and is sounding forth anew today.

"Again came the humble but firm voice: 'Whoever You wish, Lord!'

"God summoned the angel. It was Michael from one of the lowest angelic choirs. 'What makes you speak thus?'

"'Your greatness, Lord, and my nothingness.'

"At that the Lord said, 'Because you feel you are nothing in yourself, you shall wage the battle sustained by Me.'

"Borne along by the power of God, equipped with the shield of an unshakeable faith 'God is God', and girded with the sword of a burning, zealous love 'Who is like God!', the lowly servant of God plunged into a mighty battle with the proudest and most pow-

12

erful of all angels, Lucifer, the 'light bearer', the first to be created, and expelled him from the presence of God, casting him and his followers into the depths."

According to one Church tradition, Michael became the "guardian of the threshold", God's advocate, because during Lucifer's rebellion against God he stood on guard before God's throne with drawn sword, declaring, "Who is like God!"

The above legend may help us to see more clearly the origin of demonic, satanic attacks. Lucifer, failing to achieve the goal of his pride and ambition to be like God, was cast down from his exalted position; and after his rebellion the apostate angelic prince became Satan or the devil. He is also known as the evil one, the dragon, the adversary, the deceiver, the liar, the destroyer, i.e. Apollyon, who is the angel of the bottomless pit (Revelation 9:11 AV), the prince of this world, the accuser — names with dire implications and evoking dread. Satan is the invisible opponent of God. In heaven, on earth, in all creation he is the antagonist of God.

War had broken out between light and darkness, good and evil. The other angels that turned apostate with Lucifer became demons, roving spirits, who were cast out from the presence of God after failing to stand the hour of trial when the great split occurred. It could well be that on that occasion a third of the angels were expelled from their divinely appointed spheres of activity (Revelation 12:4). The apostle Peter writes about this shattering event: "God did not spare the angels when they sinned, but cast them into hell and committed them to pits of nether gloom to be kept until the judgment" (2 Peter 2:4).

Since then the kingdom of God has faced violent

opposition from Satan's realm of darkness and his hordes of demons, who as his subjects join forces with him in fighting against the light. But even if Satan and the other fallen angels have a diabolical power in this battle against the light, theirs is a broken power. When Satan overstepped the God-given boundaries between the creature and the Creator God by wanting to be like God, his personality was shattered. His vocation as the "light bearer" came to an end, and his light turned to darkness.

From the foundation of the earth God intended to have a relationship of mutual love and trust with the beings He created. But now this highly personal relationship was destroyed. Lucifer rebelled against God with his presumptuous "I am who I am; I want to be like God!" With the destruction of this perfect relationship, darkness, despair and death entered the scene. That was inevitable. Only where there is a voluntary, love-inspired dependence upon God, can there be nobility of character and divine life. With his self-assertion and rebellion Lucifer destroyed this love relationship with God and became a broken personality. Every being created by God exists solely on the current of life proceeding from the source of all life, which is and always shall be God. Only when his will is one with God, is he strong. Thus the moment Lucifer opposed God, he fell from his position of total unity with Him and lost his power as the "light bearer". He was separated from the source of life, and no more divine life flowed into him.

Satan now had to face up to the fact that there was no more divine power in him; no longer did he possess unified strength; everything that gave him authority was gone. This makes him rage to the present day, and in his malice and fury he continually attacks

14

God and all that is divine. His power has been dashed to pieces and a hideous caricature is all that remains of the fullness of light, life and love that he once possessed.

The light of God bathes one in warmth. But the light that Lucifer emanates is harsh, chilling, yes, terrifying. It does not impart life but kills. It is a travesty of light.

Moreover, since his fall Lucifer is a distorted image of life, and therefore the life he offers is a sham. He has lost the divine life that comes from union with God and that brings happiness and harmony. Ever since Lucifer rebelled against God and broke away from Him, the life within him has been characterized by disharmony and despair. This has been reflected time and again — above all, nowadays — in various lifestyles and forms of artistic and musical expression inspired by him. Everything that Satan offers in the way of life, joy and pleasure bears the imprint of death, because it is detached from God and His commandments. It contains the seeds of death and often leads to suicide. And in the next world Satan's power of death continues to have its outworking. When Jesus speaks of the "second death", this presumably consists of a continual dying process in Satan's realm.

Furthermore, as a distorted image of the divine love that Lucifer used to reflect in his role as the "light bearer", he now manifests a burning hatred, which destroys and kills and makes people's lives a misery. Ever since his fall Lucifer has raged against everything that opposes his will and rule.

This hatred is continually nourished by the great disappointment that he can never be like God, though his one consuming desire is to be like Him.

15

When Lucifer comes into the world as the Antichrist, he will compel everyone to worship him, for, to quote Luther, he apes Jesus Christ. He imitates but in the negative sense, for he lives a lie. At his prompting his followers worship him with the words, "Who is like the beast!" (Revelation 13:4), in imitation of the worshipping hosts in heaven, who cry, "Who is like God!" Again Lucifer tries to usurp the throne of God just as he did at his original fall. He is virtually consumed with the delusion "to be like God", and in his desperate struggle to attain his goal he vents all his fury on God.

Lucifer's fury against God is naturally directed against man too. Seething with envy, he hates man with every fibre of his being. Satan has lost his place at the throne once and for all; but man, whom he despises as an inferior creature made from the dust of the ground, has the opportunity of being transformed into the image of God by virtue of Jesus' act of redemption. Those who overcome will be granted vast power at the throne of God, power that Satan has lost. How he hates those who love God! He begrudges them a love relationship with God and communion with the Holy Trinity, having lost this most blessed state himself.

Determined not to let anyone attain this blessed state, he plans his attacks and assaults with great cunning and care. As we can see from the Fall, Satan plants in man the lust for power and greatness, which is his own all-consuming desire: "When you eat of it [the tree]...you will be like God" (Genesis 3:5). Because Satan had to pay for his pride by losing his place at the throne, he is determined that man too should forfeit the throne. He incites man to exalt himself by making him rebel against God and all authority.

16

To this day the "ruler of this world" (John 14:30) uses the same deceptive arguments, advocating a free autonomous personality. "Self-assertion", "power and prestige", "the freedom to do whatever one pleases" are his slogans. Woe betide us if we join in this rebellion of Lucifer, in this satanic spirit! Hubris (self-elevation and insolent pride), the presumptuous desire to be like God, turns man into a distorted image of what God created him to be. In this spirit of rebellion we ally ourselves with the first of all rebels, Satan, and lapse from a personal love relationship with God as he did. O let us not increase the grief of the Lord, who since the fall of Lucifer and the fall of man has suffered many times over as apostasy repeats itself in countless lives.

For each one of us today it is vital that we make a clean break with all satanic pride and spirit of rebellion and make an act of dedication to walk in humility and complete submission to God's will. Then all of Satan's raging against us will be in vain, for his is a broken power. Indeed, it is always shattered whenever it meets with the omnipotence and love of God, even though Satan, infuriated by his lack of power, continually leads his demons in attacks against God and those who belong to Him. Satan's plans always come to naught, for God's plans alone are valid. The love of God is greater than the power of Satan, and the blood of Jesus mightier than all the attacks of the evil one.

2
The Demons' Heyday

The world of demons, fallen angels, is very real — a fact we need to know. We have to face up to this terrible reality, so that we do not fall unsuspectingly into their hands and come under their tyranny. Nowadays Satan is manifesting his power on a grand scale, as Holy Scripture prophesies regarding the end times (Revelation 12:12). With his demons he is finding willing tools among mankind as never before. Yes, things have reached the point where Satan is worshipped in Christian countries: with growing frequency black masses are being held openly in the United States, Britain, West Germany and elsewhere.

We have entered a time when Satan and his demon hosts are celebrating their heyday. So-called Christian nations are more or less under his control. He has succeeded in inducing a large part of mankind to drink from the Harlot's cup (Revelation 17:4), which is filled to the brim with sexual filth and sorcery. (According to the Greek word used for "sorcery" in Revelation 18:23, this can also be interpreted as a striking allusion to drugs.) And it is the Harlot of Babylon who, in collaboration with the Antichrist (Revelation 17:3), seeks to lead mankind into destruction.

In our times we see that Satan has adopted a completely new and unprecedented policy. Since the Enlightenment Satan has been more or less successful in spreading the belief that he does not exist. Until the mid-sixties demonism was wrapped in secrecy. Many were unaware of its activities, which were usually carried on clandestinely. Occult happenings took place under the seal of secrecy and at night under the cover of darkness. Amulets, for instance, were worn secretly. Magic spells were cast in secret. Countless numbers suffered agonies, not realizing that they were being attacked by demonic forces. Out of shame or fear or under threat of vengeance everything was kept in the dark. And whenever people were chained to Satan, sunk in vice and depravity, they carried on their sinful activities covertly, for instance, in the privacy of a night club.

Today, however, the screen has been removed, and wickedness flaunts itself openly. The whole network of vice and demonism has surfaced and is now visible to all. This may have to do with the fact that even now the "shaft of the bottomless pit" (Revelation 9:1) has been opened to some extent. We have entered the end-time era when the earth becomes the scene for the apocalyptic battle: Satan and his demons versus God and His angels. Just how far the forces of evil and demonism have come into the open is evident from the following facts:

With complete freedom demonic forces are peddling sex in the mass media. People are urged to give free rein to their carnal desires and to reach out for pornography and perverted sexual activity — the wine of immorality, as Revelation puts it. In addition, there is the rising tide of drug addiction. More and more youngsters, yes, even children, are taking drugs.

Nowadays, with great audacity, evil is raising its

19

ugly head everywhere. It is not just certain cinemas that are showing films on heinous crimes and depraved forms of sex; nor are the mushrooming sex shows alone in what they offer to their patrons; today demons are feeding people with crude pornography and brutal violence in their own living rooms as they sit watching television. Sex has infiltrated not only trashy reading material but also serious, informative magazines as well as books released by well-known publishing houses.

A permissive life, free from all restraint in sexual matters, is not the only thing that Satan and his demons are blatantly offering. On the market they have something else, which is being heralded everywhere as a new insight. Under the slogan of a "free and autonomous personality" the theory is advanced of God-detached man who sets up his own standards and no longer has to acknowledge any authority — not even God. Consequently he can shake off the "yoke of the commandments", for he alone decides what is right and wrong. He can do as he pleases and whatever will boost his ego and gratify his desires.

True, this urge has always existed among mankind, but usually it was to be found only in individuals or isolated groups. Today there is a world-wide trend to dismiss the commandments of God as irrelevant — something that has never happened before. The result is that people feel free to sin without a twinge of conscience. Having been sanctioned by society, evil practices can now be carried on overtly and without any sense of shame: it is no longer necessary to cover them up. But this means that Satan has us on a chain, for sin and Satan belong together. Whenever we sin, Satan has a right to us unless we repent, bring our sin to the cross of Jesus, and turn from our sinful ways.

Nowadays the great power of the demons and the extensive influence they wield over people are manifest for all to see, and so too the consequences.

Gratification of every desire is what the demons offer, but emptiness and impoverishment of the soul are the result. This dehumanization of the personality accounts for the rise in crime; the growing suicide rate; the fear psychoses. Those who have accepted the demons' offer — and this goes especially for our young people — show a lack of ideals and initiative and an inability to cope with life. One result is repression, which in turn produces many psychiatric cases, even among children. Acceptance of the demons' offer results in not only emptiness and fear but utter despair. These are typical characteristics of today's youth. And the more they retreat to an escapist world of drugs, the more abysmal is their despair.

This profound sadness can be seen in the many who have given free rein to their carnal desires and are wallowing in depravity. Not only are they desperately unhappy, but they are brutal and revolutionary. At the same time they are enslaved and anything but free and independent beings. Having no opinion of their own, they are easily manipulated and follow the crowd. What is it that influences them and shapes their minds? We have only to think of the ghostly appearance of villages at night where the bluish, shimmering light of the television set shines from the windows.

Satan, the foe of human happiness, has largely achieved his objective in our times. People are drinking from his poisonous cup of sex and drugs, which causes physical sickness and very often death. He has succeeded in destroying the body. Equally successful is his work of destroying the soul. Dulled, yes, even

21

deadened, by sexual immorality and no longer receiving wholesome nourishment, the soul is reduced to a state of emptiness, misery and despair.

The spirit of man, his personality, is also being destroyed. He who succumbs to Satan's deception and only seeks to boost his ego and live as a "free", autonomous man often ends up with a fragmented personality. Isolated in his ego, he languishes in loneliness, self-impoverishment and spiritual death. Detached from God, he lacks the inflow of everlasting life, which is to be found in God alone; and seeking a substitute, he reaches out for drugs. Once again Satan achieves his objective. The victims of his work of destruction often commit suicide or end up in mental hospitals. The term "free personality" has a hollow ring to it when we think of such fragmented personalities confined to mental institutions.

Yet much to the triumph of the demons, people are blind to the reality of the demonic world. They have lost their ability to perceive demons, so that the latter can operate without fear of being detected. People are blind not only to the power and influence of demonic forces but to the hideousness of sin and its fatal results. They are unaware that all this is part of a campaign from hell led by Lucifer, who claims that he is able to satisfy people's hunger for life. But the life he offers is a poisonous draught bringing death. They do not realize that they are being denied the greatest joy and most precious thing there is to be had: true love, which is being replaced by Lucifer's offer of sex. Nor do people see that Satan's proposal for humanistic socio-political involvement actually robs them of true brotherly love. For what is love based on socio-political humanism? — love without a heart. It aims at changing the structure of society, if need be through violence, and thus it breeds hatred, revolt, murder and utter misery. It quenches true brotherly love, which takes a warm, personal interest in one's neighbour, caring for him in a sacrificial spirit when he is in distress. How apt is Jesus' prophecy for the end times: "Most men's love will grow cold" (Matthew 24:12)!

The majority of mankind today, especially in the West, do not realize that Satan is just luring them on with the promise of developing a free personality. It is a bait. From of old Satan has been a liar, bent on leading mankind into misery. But man is blind to Satan's evil intentions; he does not see that Satan seeks to destroy him by separating him from God. Satan knows that God created man to enjoy a highly personal relationship with his Maker — a relationship of mutual love. And he knows that once man is detached from the source of divine life he will fall into his clutches.

Dazzled by the false light of the liar, people think that God wants to force them into accepting His rule. They do not realize that God has given them complete freedom either to commit themselves to Him or not. God is Love and He longs for genuine love in return — a voluntary love. Yes, Satan leads people astray, so that they no longer realize that love for God and dependence upon Him actually bring them joy and ennoble them. They no longer see that whenever man severs himself from God, whenever he oversteps the boundary between creature and Maker and seeks to be on a par with God, his personality deteriorates. Where this ultimately leads to we can see from the German philosopher Nietzsche, who died a lunatic. People do not realize that behind all the new slogans, the new insights, the "new morality" there lies a strategic plan of Satan, which in our times seems to be coming to fruition.

People do not see Satan's cleverly devised plan to destroy divine precepts and to create a diabolical chaos by undermining the laws and ethics of a nation concerning marriage, family life, and moral behaviour between the sexes.

It seems as though Satan has taken counsel together with his demons and in great fury has worked out a plan for our times. No longer are the demons giving all their attention to certain restricted areas of life where sin had always triumphed — for example, concentration camps, the underworld, gambling casinos, occult meetings, fortune-tellers' sessions and night clubs. Now the time has come when the demons are flooding the whole earth and every area of life. Their attack is wide-ranging and not just limited to particular sections of society.

Nor is that all. What makes Satan's present-day tactics so unique is that the demons have invaded the Church in order to destroy it. They have managed to gain a foothold within the realm of church life. Never before in the history of the Church of Jesus Christ has there been a situation like this.

The plan to destroy the Church was launched by declaring the concept of sin to be outdated and by making Jesus redundant as the Saviour of sinners and Redeemer of mankind. Because social evils, and not sin, were dealt with as the root of man's troubles, Jesus was declared to be a social reformer, and the Christian world in general veered towards humanistic socialism. The emphasis was shifted. For many Christians, Jesus was no longer the centre of their lives. They no longer gave Him their love and the honour that is His due. Their attention was focused

24

on man instead. Not only was love for Jesus quenched in millions, but there was a gradual falling away from the faith and from a life of discipleship.

The demons hold sway particularly over those church groups which issue the slogans of a brotherly love that has nothing to do with God. Ultimately this so-called love leads to the glorification of sex, for sex is considered to be essential for a fulfilled life. This is why many theologians justify premarital sex and appeal for tolerance towards deviant sexual behaviour.

A change in the structure of society, if need be through violence, is also presented under the cloak of Christianity as being the remedy for mankind's ills. Even believers are being deceived today by the demons with their dazzling, beguiling light, which is taken for the true light of knowledge. "A new age needs a new morality." "We can no longer be expected to adhere to the commandments of God in this new age of freedom and self-realization for man." "The constraint of the commandments and the whole concept of authority must go, so that we can develop our potential freely and find our true identity." Believers are being challenged with arguments like these even from the pulpit.

Imperceptibly the demons have already gained control over many believers. After indoctrinating people with the idea that authority must go, they then take control of them, laughing scornfully. Free personalities with the right to decide for themselves become slaves, who must do as their master says. They are subject to a cruel authority, the authority of Satan. Now they have to do what he wants. For instance, some have the compulsion to take drugs even if this leads to mental derangement or death. They have actually lost the freedom that Satan, the liar, dangled before them in his tempting bait of a new morality and new insights. Under the rule of God they would have had true freedom. Instead of slaves they would have been voluntary servants of love living in a highly personal relationship with God, their Maker and Father, who does not lead His children into misery, death and ruin, but fills their lives with joy and happiness.

Now they are slaves. But although they can sense their fetters, they do not realize in whose grip they are, because they deny and even scoff at the existence of Satan and his demons. They are captives of the devil, ensnared to do his will, as Paul writes in 2 Timothy 2:26.

Since all this leads to despair and death, people who face reality and want to honour the truth really ought to admit that they incurred misery because they were led astray by deceitful arguments — false, beguiling lights. But although Satan stands unmasked before our eyes as the liar from of old, many who normally pay attention to the facts and adjust their lives accordingly are blind in this respect.

While millions in so-called Christian countries are falling prey to Satan's wiles today, he is also persecuting believers with greater fury than ever before. This century has seen more Christians tortured and killed for their faith than any other century. Satan and his servants, the fallen angels or demons, are celebrating their heyday, for we have entered the end times when, as Jesus prophesied, all these things would take place.

For Satan and his demons the final chapter in history, preceding the return of Jesus Christ, is their last great chance to extend their kingdom and to turn large numbers into their slaves. Thus they are con-

26

centrating their activities on an all-out effort to make the most of the remaining time. They want to have in their kingdom many subjects, whom they can rule over and torment. A comparison can be made with concentration camps. Inspired by hell, the overseers often gloated with a diabolical joy when the barracks were refilled with prisoners — thousands of new victims on whom they could practise their sadism.

In the hour of death the servants of Satan will find themselves face to face with him and the demons in all their hideousness. Then they will realize under whose dominion they had been when they yielded to temptation and served the forces of darkness. Satan will torment them as his slaves in his kingdom of horrors, to which Jesus often referred. In this life too Satan torments his slaves, though only to a limited extent. Even so, this gives us an inkling of the torments that await people in the next world, in Satan's realm, where there is darkness and anguish, wailing and gnashing of teeth. May we ever bear in mind this frightening reality, seeing that we live in an age when Satan and his demons are staging their major onslaught.

3
Combat with Satan Today

Since we are living in the heyday of these evil spirits, the demons, we need to be more alert than ever. The end-time battle of the spirits is on and no one can avoid being involved, for we, mankind, are the target of Satan and his demons. The battle is being waged over us. Our eternal destiny is at stake.

This calls for action, an all-out effort on our part. By placing us in this situation, God is challenging us to pray and battle in faith as never before. Holy Scripture exhorts us, "Put on the whole armour of God, that you may be able to stand against the wiles of the devil. For we do not wrestle against flesh and blood, but against principalities, against powers, against the rulers of the darkness of this age, against spiritual hosts of wickedness in the heavenly places" (Ephesians 6:11f. RAV). Today this is a must for everyone who belongs to Jesus.

We enter this battle knowing of the immense power and influence of Satan, who is unremitting in his efforts to make us unhappy here and, after our life is over, to carry us off into his kingdom of darkness as his booty. But we also know that Satan is limited in his actions. Jesus Christ, and not he, is Lord.

What a triumph! At Calvary Satan was judged, and with him his demons: "Now is the judgment of this world, now shall the ruler of this world be cast out" (John 12:31). The first stage of judgment has

28

taken place. Satan has been deprived of his rights. However, he has not yet been bound in prison (that is, the bottomless pit); nor has he been cast into the lake of fire and brimstone (Revelation 20). He is still the prince of this world. As a fallen, disentitled angelic prince he can still assail us with temptations and deceive us if we are not on the alert and battling against him in the strength of Jesus' outpoured blood.

Ever anew we need to confront the fact that we have an enemy, an archenemy. A murderer from the beginning, he persecutes us with a burning hatred, no doubt assigning to each one of us a specific demon or a number of them in order to achieve his objective. As the destroyer he wants to blight our prospects of true joy. He seeks to ruin body, soul and spirit if we but give him an opening. This occurs when we abandon ourselves to sin, as is so often the case nowadays when the commandments of God are declared invalid and many people no longer take them seriously. On the other hand, Satan as the great antagonist of God retaliates every single time the kingdom of God makes an advance. In the council sessions of hell he continually hatches plots with his demons – every day anew – and has an excellent strategy with which he launches his attacks. He knows the chink in every person's armour: arrogance, love of the world, attachment to earthly things, carnal desires, love of money, envy, bitterness, and so on.

The New Testament warns us of Satan's intentions, devices and schemes. It urges us to size up our enemy, so that we can fight against him successfully and thus "keep Satan from gaining the advantage over us; for we are not ignorant of his designs" (2 Corinthians 2:11). But which of us is actually conscious that enticement to sin is more than a passing whim? Behind every temptation is a very real personality, who is bent on causing our downfall. We tend to look superficially at things, failing to realize that all the time an enemy is lurking in the background and doing everything possible to make us fall in one way or another. We do not take into account how gruesome, how cruel, Satan and his demons are. In the final analysis we do not seriously believe that they are right beside us, plying us with subtle arguments and engineering circumstances and events in our lives, all with a view to ensnaring us.

Yes, Satan wants to destroy something of our God-given personality by enticing us to sin. And after sin has done its work in us, he will take us into his kingdom of horrors as his rightful subjects. There as the tormentor he will vent his malice on us and torture us. If he does not succeed in carrying us off to his kingdom, he will at least try to prevent us from reaching the goal of the City of God.

Whoever is off his guard nowadays, that is, whoever is ignorant of the tactics and intentions of his opponent Satan and the demons, will be caught unawares. Somehow or other he will be taken in by Satan's arguments. He will accept the easy way out that the evil one offers him. This we see happening with regard to the seventh commandment, which upholds the sanctity of marriage. In our times this commandment is being rejected by a permissive society, which promotes premarital and extramarital relationships. We also see it happening with regard to the commandment to honour our parents, to obey them and others in authority. Some consider the path of humility and submission to be fit only for weaklings, but in reality it is the path of the strong. It takes courage and strength of character to be humble. Every path that has the commandments of God for guideposts is a path of love, which we follow of our own free will; it fully develops our personalities and ennobles them. But if we listen to Satan's arguments about a free personality and follow his path, it will lead us to destruction. Even so, these stratagems of Satan and his demons continue to meet with success.

"Why does God allow us to be exposed to such temptations?" is a question many ask themselves. Demons are instrumental in God's plans; He allows them to tempt us so that we shall be tried and tested. God does not want us to be slaves. He wants us to give ourselves to Him with a voluntary love. This is why He gives us freedom of choice. No one need succumb to Satan's temptations. The one who takes the shield of faith and resists Satan will experience that Satan flees from him and God draws near (James 4:7f.). Yes, he will be numbered among the overcomers and given a crown in heaven.

In order to wage a proper battle of faith against the forces of evil, we first need to acknowledge that demons exist. Everything depends upon this. If I do not face up to the fact that I have an enemy, I shall be an easy prey for him. But if we reckon with the reality of the demons, it follows that we shall be filled with great wrath towards them. Then we shall start battling against them with all our might. We are all involved in this spiritual warfare, and our eternal destiny depends on whether we win or lose. He who does not battle will fall into Satan's snares and come to ruin. Wishing to protect us from this fate, Jesus repeatedly warns us by showing us how endangered we are — especially as believers. We shall fall prey to Satan if, for instance, we live in unforgiveness, hold a

31

grudge against someone, or do not respect the sanctity of marriage. In the parable of the unforgiving servant Jesus says that he is delivered "to the torturers" (Matthew 18:34 RAV), and elsewhere He says that the whole body can be cast into hell as a result of impure desires (Matthew 5:27-30).

The reality of Satan and his demons is especially evident nowadays in the lives of those who have accepted his offer, choosing to exalt their ego and live a life of unrestrained pleasure by indulging in sex, drugs and so forth. We have already spoken about the troubles and misery they experienced as a result. Natural explanations may be found in some cases; however, it is no longer possible to explain everything on natural grounds once we look at the realm of the occult. When people consciously give themselves to Satan or when they come under his power through incantations or what they consider to be innocent pastimes: table-turning, fortune-telling, séances, ouija boards, tarot cards and astrology, to list but a few examples — they invite the forces of evil into their lives.

Factual accounts bear this out:

On the porch of a mission-building in India a man stood and coughed as a sign that he wanted to talk with the missionary. It was one of his evangelists, and with a trembling voice he reported:

"Sir, stones keep dropping inside our house — ghost stones. Every evening after sundown the spooky thing begins. We close the doors and windows, but the stones keep dropping. This has been going on now for two weeks. We don't have any peace. Sir, please come and help us."

When the missionary arrived in the

evangelist's house after sundown, he learnt that on that evening the mysterious occurrence had begun two hours earlier. While they sat in the room with the windows closed a stone dropped, then another and another. Where did they come from? It was impossible that they came from outside. Did they perhaps fall through the ceiling? But how did they get into the house in the first place? The missionary climbed up a ladder to take a look. The ceiling was black with soot from the open fireplace. If the stones had fallen through the ceiling, they must be sooty. The missionary carefully examined everything but found nothing. There he stood, the clever white man, who had learnt that such a thing was scientifically impossible. Yet with his own eyes he could see it happening — and so could the others.

The missionary called the household together for evening devotions, choosing as his theme the first chapter in the Gospel of Mark, which tells of Jesus casting out demons. During the devotions all was quiet. Then the stones began to drop again. The missionary rebuked the evil spirits in the name of Jesus, but to no avail.

With a troubled heart the missionary retired for the night. Christ must have the victory over this house. But how? There must be something wrong in the evangelist's life, giving the evil spirits a platform from which to operate. The next morning the missionary talked with the evangelist about his unfaithfulness in handling money matters. The evangelist, conscience-stricken, took his words to heart and promised to mend his ways. And — oh, what a marvel it was! — a whole week passed by without any stones falling. Then they started dropping again. So it was plain that there was something else behind these happenings; and until that was brought to light and removed, the spell would continue to be effective and cause disturbances. But what was it that still lay hidden?

When the missionary was on his way again to this village, a young candidate for baptism related the following while carrying his luggage for him: About one-and-a-half years ago the evangelist's predecessor, who had lived in the same house where the stones kept falling, had called the witch doctor from the neighbouring village to heal his son. After the magic rites were over, they had buried the magic instruments to the east of the house.

That afternoon the missionary went with the present evangelist to find the place where the demonic utensils were buried. After searching a while, they found the spot; and unearthing the magic instruments, they prayed and destroyed them. With that, the whole matter was cleared up and no more stones dropped.[1]

Not only in the pagan environment of India but also in our so-called Christian country people have experienced the reality of demonic power. There is an account about a man who had turned to Satan for help.[2]

During an evangelistic crusade this demon-oppressed man told his story in the presence of the pastor, a church elder, and his cousin.

In the year 1935 he wanted to marry. Neither he nor his fiancée could meet the expense of a room. In a tavern an acquaintance advised him,

"Make a contract with the devil asking him for 500 Marks and write it with your own blood. Place the contract on the table at midnight and call three times in the darkened room, 'Lucifer, come!'"

The young man followed this piece of advice. He cut his finger and wrote a petition for 500 Marks with the pledge to give his soul in exchange. At midnight he called three times, "Lucifer, come!"

All of a sudden an uncanny feeling came over him. Above him he saw a pair of gleaming red eyes. Then a pale hand reached across the table. The horrified man turned on the light. There on the table lay a wad of bank notes, adding up to 500 Marks. The first piece of paper was gone and instead there was a new piece of paper with the words, "Be at the crossroads at the top of the village tomorrow at midnight."

From that point on the man felt very uneasy. He decided not to go to the crossroads on the following night. However, as the second evening drew near, he was seized with a great inner compulsion to go after all. Pocketing his revolver, he set out.

At the crossroads he saw a hideous figure — half man, half beast. He fired all the cartridges at the creature, which then disappeared before his eyes.

For the man himself the most puzzling part was that he still had the 500 Marks and no one came to demand the money back, saying that the whole thing was a joke. He paid for the room and got married. But he could never shake off the uneasiness he felt since receiving the money. There were often times when he had the feeling that he was being pursued by the Furies. He began to have a haunted look about him, his face became lined, and his hair turned white. At the age of forty-three when he made his confession he looked like a seventy-year-old.

During the confession, which lasted two-and-a-half hours, the four men were startled from time to time by tapping on the window. Oddly enough, although the wooden shutters were closed, the tapping was not the muffled sound of wood being tapped, but that of a window pane. In spite of his confession the agitated man did not lose his restlessness.

In our part of the world there are also accounts about the power and influence of demons in the lives of people who did not actually have any dealings with the occult but happened to live in a house where there had been occult practices, which opened the way for evil spirits to make that house their dwelling-place and sphere of influence.

A young pastor was transferred to a parish with a low church-attendance. The Word of God meant little to the villagers. Instead, all kinds of superstitious practices were prevalent: hypnotism, tarot cards and curing by incantation. The young pastor did not feel at ease in his new parish. In the parsonage strange observations were made that could not be explained rationally. Time and again the young wife said to her husband that there was something uncanny about the house, but the pastor would dismiss the thought with a laugh: "Nonsense, it's just a lot of hocus-pocus."

One night, however, a strange occurrence

forced him to concern himself with these goings-on. The baby, which was lying in its cot next to the parents' bedroom, suddenly began to scream in terror. The young mother rushed through the open door to the adjoining room to calm the child. But she started back in horror and called her husband. Both parents saw that the diaper had been removed from the child, which now lay in the reverse direction in its cot with bruises on its body as though a hand had gripped it.

At first the pastor thought it was an impudent hoax. He carefully tested the window catches, as well as the lock of the other door in the bedroom leading into the hall, and shone the flashlight into every corner of the room. The diaper was also examined for a possible cause of the scratches and bruises. However, the parents did not find a single clue. The mother tucked the baby in its cot and calmed it. Then the parents went back to bed.

Again the frightening screams and whimpering began. Together the parents rushed into the adjoining room, where the infant lay in the reverse direction in its cot with its diaper removed. Its tiny body once again showed traces of a violent grip with the typical marks of a human hand. Filled with an eerie sensation, the couple took the baby with them to bed. The husband, seeking for some explanation, commented to his wife, "It does seem that there are strange goings-on here."

...By now he was almost convinced that there was something wrong with the parsonage. What was behind it all he did not know, but secretly he began to hunt for a clue that would help him to get to the bottom of these puzzling happenings.

An elderly church warden came to his assistance. In a confidential talk he revealed that for twenty-eight years a spiritistic group had met at the parsonage with the former pastor, who had experimented with the occult.[3]

Whenever the fallen angels, Satan and his demons, exert their influence over people, they torment them. And down through the centuries they have been especially able to exert their influence when people give Satan and his demons a right to them by contacting them. Horoscope-reading, table-turning, fortune-telling and healing by pious-sounding but sinister incantations are some of the means by which this can happen. How many people — including those who call themselves believers — have come under demonic influence by dabbling in what they considered to be harmless activities! Nowadays the number is escalating. Incredible though it may seem, records at the Inland Revenue Department in West Germany show that at the time of writing there are twice as many registered sorcerers, palmists and fortune-tellers (and how many unregistered ones are there?) as ministers and priests in this country. In Paris there is one sorcerer for every 120 citizens, whereas one doctor for every 520 citizens, and one clergyman for every 5,000 citizens. It is not surprising that even among believers an alarming percentage have dealings with the occult.

Such people can find no inner peace. They have an aversion to the Word of God and prayer, and suffer from spiritual paralysis, doubts, fears and depression even to the point of thinking blasphemous thoughts and contemplating suicide. Symptoms like these can be traced back to occult practices in their personal or family backgrounds, as talks with spiritual counsellors reveal.

There are areas where it is common practice even for Christians to make use of occult treatment when sickness strikes. For instance, they take their sick children to a woman in the village to be cured by a charm or incantation. The consequences are serious, for in this way Satan is given a claim to a person's life. A young girl of a devout Christian family told me that during a serious illness in her childhood she was taken by her mother to such a woman, as was usual in the whole area. To all appearances she was cured, but from that time onwards she was tormented by evil spirits. Scarcely a night passed by when she was not harassed by them. The disturbances they caused were so real that the lamps were often hanging askew the next morning, loud noises could be heard coming from the room, and on her body she bore traces of these tormenting experiences. And so this girl lived in constant dread of these evil spirits until she experienced the releasing and protecting power of Jesus' blood.

From the above examples we have a glimpse of the unnerving reality of Satan. Together with his demons he is at our heels, especially today, eager to lay claim to us and bring us under his dominion in order to destroy us for ever. This burning hatred of Satan and the demons as they rage to gain control over us is a challenge for every believer to enter into spiritual warfare as never before. We need to give the right response by taking the offensive and waging genuine battles of faith in our prayers. We have been given an effective weapon to defeat the enemy, a weapon that never fails to hit the mark and ward off his blows.

This weapon is the prayer of faith, in which we, metaphorically speaking, hurl the victorious name of Jesus at Satan. Whoever calls upon the name of Jesus in faith, trusting in Him, the crucified and risen Lord, the triumphant Lamb of God, will find that the enemy cannot succeed in his attacks against him. Here it is a matter of applying the words of the apostle Paul: "Take up the shield of faith, with which you can extinguish all the flaming arrows of the evil one" (Ephesians 6:16 NIV).

However, it is not enough to call upon the name of Jesus just once. The enemy does not usually yield that quickly. A war consists of many battles. If we have won one battle, Satan or the demon he has assigned to us is busy preparing the next onslaught. But if we should then fail to resume the battle of faith because we have grown tired of having to fight all the time, we are lost. Then we are already in the hands of the enemy. Whoever does not resist him is like a soldier who does not defend himself when attacked. Without fail he will be taken captive. Perseverance is what counts in the battle of faith.

Thus the watchword for the end times is, "Here is a call for the endurance and faith of the saints" (Revelation 13:10). This is a faith that perseveres in patience, that takes its stand on God's promises and Jesus' victory at Calvary and ever anew uses the weapon of Jesus' name in words like the following, "Jesus has broken the devil's might. The Lamb of God has won the fight!" Let us confront Satan ever anew with the victory of Jesus by praising the victorious name of Jesus and His precious blood in manifold ways. If we do not grow weary but persevere and battle in faith for ourselves or others, we shall experience a great and far-reaching victory. Every new onslaught of Satan as well as every seeming defeat should be taken as a challenge to battle all the more in prayer and faith, so that the victory of Jesus can be demonstrated on an even greater scale.

The prerequisites laid down by Holy Scripture are not only patience and faith but keeping the commandments of God (Revelation 14:12). In the first letter of John this connection between answered prayers and the keeping of the commandments is clearly shown: "We receive from him whatever we ask, because we keep his commandments and do what pleases him" (1 John 3:22). In other words, our prayers will have power to overcome the stratagems of Satan when prayer hindrances such as disobedience to God's commandments are removed. This means making a break with the sins and iniquities that stand between God and us and prevent Him from answering our prayers.

This does not mean, however, that we have to be sinless if God is to answer our prayers in the battle against the demons. We are sinners until the day we die, for we sin again and again. However, when we tolerate our besetting sins, persist in them, do not hate them, nor want to "pluck out our eye", we are separated from God and have no power in the battle of faith against Satan. Everyone who commits sin willingly, gives himself to Satan and binds himself to him. Could there be a greater discrepancy than attempting to fight against the evil one while still serving sin? Satan will laugh scornfully and bind the hypocrite all the more firmly to himself. But he who repents of his sins daily, confesses them and is cleansed in the blood of the Lamb will experience that the greater the battle against sin and satanic powers, the greater the victory.

This applies especially to our intercession for the deliverance of people who because of their involvement in the occult have come under the power of Satan and cannot get free. What a battle it is when we try to help them to renounce all contact with the powers of darkness, to receive Jesus anew and to call upon His name! But at the name of Jesus chains of sin are burst asunder and Satan flees. Time and again this is demonstrated in the lives of young drug addicts who have been set free from these satanic bonds by calling upon the name of Jesus. Yes, even in cases of demon possession the words hold true: "There is Someone who has destroyed Satan's power — Jesus Christ on the cross at Calvary."

Living in China was a young girl who became demon-possessed. While on leave, her brother, a Red Guard, was shocked to see the change in his pretty, vivacious sister of a year ago. Looking like an old hag, she glanced wildly about her, her face agonized and distorted. A man's voice spoke with her lips, "There is only one I fear, only one — Jesus of Nazareth!"

Deeply troubled, the young Chinese sought to trace the whereabouts of this Jesus of Nazareth, who alone could help his sister. But no one in the village knew of him. Then suddenly he was reminded of an incident that had occurred earlier on his way back home. Because the bus had broken down, he was forced to make a stop in a community where he was received with great friendliness and made to feel at home. When he was about to leave, the leader said to him, "May our Lord Jesus bless you! Go your way, and His peace be with you."

The young Chinese, desperate for his sister's

sake, travelled through the night till he reached the community, for he felt this was the only place where he could hope to find help. Two men belonging to this particular Jesus' Family [one of many Christian centres in North China known as Homes, or Families, of Jesus] went back with him to help his afflicted sister.

As the men went in to see the sister, who from the moment they set foot in the house began to rave more wildly than ever, they found her sitting on the floor, her hands tangled in her hair. Like a wounded animal she stared at them with a half-crazed, bewildered look in her wide eyes.

"What do you want?" the voice bellowed from within her.

The two Christians stretched out their right hands. "Covered by the blood of Jesus, we command you in the name of Jesus, you tormenting spirit, you nameless demon, to come out of your victim. With the authority of Jesus and in His name we command you to go at once to the place that Jesus has prepared for you. There He will bind you for ever. You cannot return. For Jesus is Victor!"

Calmly and firmly they spoke word after word, sentence after sentence.

The girl writhed on the floor. From within her the man's voice replied, "I'll go," repeating, "I'll go," but then more faintly until with a series of "I'll go, I'll go, I'll…" the voice was lost in the distance.

One of the Christians went up to the girl and laid his hands on her, saying, "All power in heaven and on earth belongs to our victorious Lord Jesus, and you are under His protection, daughter. Jesus is your peace for time and eternity. Receive the Holy Spirit. May the Lord keep and guard you from all harm and evil, and may He help and strengthen you in every good work. Amen."

The girl lay there as if dead. The second man went up to her, grasped her by the hand and drew her up, saying, "Arise. Jesus is Victor! He whom the Son makes free is free indeed."

The girl's father could scarcely believe his eyes when he saw his daughter rise to her feet. After all those months the expression on her face was normal again. It was as if she had just awoken after a long deep sleep and was trying hard to remember something. A number of times she drew a deep breath. Then seeing her father among those present, she went up to him smiling. "Father," she exclaimed joyfully, "I can breathe again. I'm back with you!"[4]

The victorious might that the name of Jesus wields over the powers of darkness was also evident in the revival area in Indonesia, as Pak Oktavianus testified.[5]

The Gospel team of his Bible college was facing opposition from a well-known spiritist and sorcerer, who had already proved his magical powers. For instance, he would count to five and a hen running by would die; or he would look a dog in the eye and it would fall down dead, though when asked to bring the dog back to life he was unable to do so.

He now came to challenge us..."I tell you, I can also make people fall down dead! Who has more power — your Jesus or the masters of magic who have taught me?"

Everyone in the Bible college was driven to prayer, and the Lord gave us the assurance that we were to accept his challenge...While our Bible college fellowship prayed, the sorcerer and I sat in my office — face to face. "Look me straight in the eye," the man said. "When you do that, you too will fall down dead!" And he removed his glasses.

Sitting opposite him, I also took off my glasses and in the name of Jesus Christ I rebuked him: "In the name of Jesus Christ I bind the forces of evil in you. Today you have no power!"

Then we looked each other straight in the eye. And he slumped to the ground like a dead man, his body stiff as wood.

My Christian brothers and I then prayed together and said, "In the name of Jesus Christ, arise!"

At that he stirred. But when he got up, he was cross-eyed. "Jesus really is Lord!" he stammered.

As he gradually regained full consciousness and began to think things over, he said, "But I still have power! Twenty years ago two golden needles were placed in both my arms by magic...These are the source of my power and influence..." This power had enabled him to move about without being caught. The other two needles in his arms protected him from being hit by bullets or from being stabbed.

To one of our Bible college students he said, "Take your knife and stab me." The student did so, but the knife did not pierce his flesh. The sorcerer said, "I still have this power. Does Jesus have the power to get these golden needles out of my body?"

Once again we prayed. And the Lord gave us the assurance that He did have this power. Again we felt we had to confront the evil forces within the sorcerer. I said, "In the name of Jesus Christ I declare that these needles must come out of your body!"

The needles began to move in his body, and with our own eyes we saw them come out of his skin. There were many witnesses. Our entire Bible college fellowship testified that the needles came out of both his arms. Each time one of those needles came out, he fell down, his body stiffening like wood. We had to revive him by calling upon the name of Jesus. In the end he acknowledged that Jesus Christ really is God.

In Africa the victory of the name of Jesus over the demons has also been demonstrated. There in the heart of Angola was a missionary friend of ours, who longed for Jesus' kingdom of love to shine forth in her dark surroundings. And so it was a grief for her that Ilaque, one of their converts, could still be tormented by demonic forces. The members of the local church began to battle in prayer for him. About that time our missionary friend received a prayer from Canaan* that many have found to be very helpful: the Prayer of Victory in the Name of Jesus and in His Wounds.

Months later the missionary joyfully wrote to us, "...This 'Prayer of Victory in the Name of Jesus and in His Wounds' was a great help in the battle for Ilaque and his deliverance...Brother Ilaque has been set free, although we had almost given up believing that a miracle could occur. Through the name of

---

* *Canaan* is the name we have given to the grounds belonging to our Sisterhood, since this piece of land is meant to be a sign pointing to the coming dominion of God.

Jesus this demon-oppressed man became free and now he gives his testimony at the evangelistic meetings."

Now what are the aids for the battle against demons — whether in the case of demon possession, or in our personal struggle with demonic forces, whose attacks we and those whom we know and love are so painfully made to feel in these days? We can oppose the enemy's onslaughts by praying verses of Holy Scripture, such as:

He [Jesus Christ] disarmed the principalities
and powers and made a public example of them,
triumphing over them in him.

Colossians 2:15

The reason the Son of God appeared was to
destroy the works of the devil.

1 John 3:8

Thanks be to God, who gives us the victory
through our Lord Jesus Christ.

1 Corinthians 15:57

Hark, glad songs of victory in the tents of
the righteous: "The right hand of the Lord does
valiantly, the right hand of the Lord is
exalted."

Psalm 118:15f.

It is finished.

John 19:30

So if the Son makes you free, you will be
free indeed.

John 8:36

Jesus Christ, the living One, has "the keys of Death and Hades".

cf. Revelation 1:18

Satan and his demons are put to flight when we call upon Jesus, the triumphant Prince of Victory, who overcame the power of hell and crushed the head of the serpent.

This we can also do in song. According to St. Augustine, singing is thrice praying. In our churches and prayer fellowships we surely have our favourite hymns and songs celebrating the victory of Jesus. Or we may like to sing songs like the following:

> Let praises ring aloud this day,
> That Jesus' name has pow'r
> To break apart the fearful chains
>   of sin that bind us.
>
> Let praises ring aloud this day,
> That by this mighty name
> The powers of hell are put to flight
>   and made to tremble.
>
> When Jesus' name is loudly called,
> The gate of heav'n springs wide;
> And demons flee, for Jesus comes to
>   all who trust Him.

*

'Tis only One who has such might,
'Tis Jesus, who once won the fight
And Satan's pow'r defeated.
And still He puts the foe to flight
And takes from Satan ev'ry right,
Our living, glorious Champion.

Our ransom has been fully bought;
All Satan's wiles must come to nought;
His claims on us are cancelled.
Our souls to Christ alone belong,
Who gave His life to right all wrong,
And ransom us poor sinners.

So let us now Christ's vict'ry sing;
Let earth with shouts of triumph ring,
And force the foe's withdrawal.
The name of Jesus wields such pow'r;
The hosts of darkness can but cow'r
Before its might so awesome.
Hallelujah, Hallelujah[16]

For this battle of faith we may also like to use some
of the prayers of victory that those believers in Africa
used:
    In the name of Jesus and in His wounds
    there is victory! Jesus Christ has trod upon
    the head of the serpent and also conquered its
    power over me. The victory has been won.
                                         Hallelujah!
    In the name of Jesus and in His wounds
    there is victory! Jesus Christ has abolished
    the power of death — in my heart and life as
    well. He has overcome death.
                                         Hallelujah!

In the name of Jesus and in His wounds
there is victory! The Lamb, the Lion of Judah,
has overcome Satan's power — in my life as
well. Jesus is Victor!

Hallelujah!

In the name of Jesus and in His wounds
there is victory! Jesus has put all His
enemies under His feet — in my life as well.
The enemy has been overcome. Jesus is Victor!

Hallelujah!

In the name of Jesus and in His wounds
there is victory! Jesus has come to destroy
the works of the devil. They are destroyed,
for Jesus is Victor!

Hallelujah!

In the name of Jesus and in His wounds
there is victory! Jesus has redeemed me from
every power of sin, for He says, "If the Son
makes you free, you will be free indeed."
This truth avails for me. I have been redeemed
from my sinful bonds. Jesus is Victor!

Hallelujah!

In the name of Jesus and in His wounds
there is victory! I know that my Redeemer lives.
He redeems me and remoulds me into a new
creation. Jesus sets me free.

Hallelujah!

In the name of Jesus and in His wounds
there is victory! Jesus has disarmed His
enemies and made a public display of them.
Jesus is Victor over every power of the enemy.

Hallelujah!

In the name of Jesus and in His wounds
there is victory! Jesus has the keys of Death
and Hades. No longer can the enemy harm me,
rage as he will. I am redeemed. Jesus is Victor!

Hallelujah![7]

The more we pray and battle in faith, the more we
shall experience victory. Every new onslaught of the
enemy should serve to make us stronger in faith and
teach us to overcome. It is Satan's attacks that help us
to attain through the battle of faith the very things
that he tries to deprive us of: the crown of life and the
glory at the throne of God.

Let us remember that we are never alone in our
struggle, for God has commissioned His holy angels
to battle against the demons. How important it is for
us to know this! Imbued with tremendous power
from the throne on high, these heavenly warriors
exert all their efforts for us. This we may count on.
Indeed, we must. How can we otherwise endure in an
age when hell has set up its stronghold on earth and
we are constantly surrounded by demons and exposed to manifold temptations?

But if we battle, day by day, trusting in the victory
of Jesus and the power of His angels — ever conscious
that Satan with his demons "prowls around like a
roaring lion, seeking some one to devour" (1 Peter
5:8) — then Satan will get nowhere with his
stratagems. Though he constantly seeks to do us

harm, he will not be able to gain power over us.

By raging against us and the will of God, Satan unwittingly serves the purposes of God. As a result of his attacks people learn to persevere in faith; they grow stronger spiritually; and, having stood the test, these overcomers will one day inherit the crown of life and behold the wonderful purposes of God behind all temptations. Satan is merely instrumental in carrying out the will of God, not only in our personal lives but in God's saving work in history, as we shall see with awe in heaven above. Even now we know that Satan's raging in the end-time era and his massive display of power will lead to his crushing defeat and total conquest. The power he exerts over people will be utterly destroyed. The final Victor is Jesus, before whom every knee will bow. Satan, however, will be cast into the lake of fire, where he will burn (Revelation 20:10).

We are approaching the hour when Jesus will assume His rule over all the kingdoms of the world. Let us, therefore, live in anticipation of this hour. Let us prepare for it and withstand the devious, concentrated attacks of Satan in our times.

In order to gain the victory in this battle we, more than any other generation, need to be aware of the nature, power and ministry of the angels, who according to Holy Scripture are endowed with great might as they war against the demons on our behalf. This is their special commission in the end times. For now, as in no other time, hell is a hive of activity and busy mobilizing its demon troops. With the same intensity the hosts of holy angels, the angels of light at the throne of God, are also in motion. They are the ones who at the end of the age will join forces with Jesus in battle against the hordes of demons, utterly routing them. The holy angels fight in the name of Jesus Christ, the Victor, and so their victory is assured. Their power is a thousand times greater than that of the fallen angels, the demons, whom they will overthrow in the last battle.

What a mighty army stands ready to help us at a time when the demons are staging their major onslaught! Let us remember that these heavenly hosts are a reality and let us count on their assistance. Then we shall see that the fallen angels, the demons, are ultimately powerless. Theirs is a broken power, and despite all their raging they are no match for the angels with their unbroken divine strength.

Angels –
Heralds of God's Greatness

The present age, demonized as no other age, denies the existence of demons. The present age, in which the angels have entered into the final conflict, also denies the existence of angels. When rationalism and liberalism made their début, this attitude began to take root, making it possible for a theologian like Schleiermacher to declare, "The only thing that can be set forward as a doctrine concerning the angels is this: Whether or not angels exist should not have any influence on our conduct, and visitations of angels are no longer to be expected" (*Glaubenslehre* II, par.33).[8]

In our times, however, this demythologization has permeated many areas of church life with devastating effects.

We pride ourselves on our intelligence and progressiveness, but how foolish we are. At great loss to our spiritual lives we ignore the reality of the angels, which are referred to by Holy Scripture in nearly 300 places. If only we realized what divine riches God has in store for us. At a time when the Holy Spirit is demonstrating afresh the living reality of Jesus Christ through revivals, may He also help us to see again the reality of the Lord's holy angels, who glorify Him.

4
Angels —
A Reflection of God's Glory

We long to know God better, the great, omnipotent, eternal and thrice-holy God, the Lord of all aeons, who reigns supreme over all worlds, who has all power and might, who dwells in an inapproachable light, who alone is eternal and immortal. And we shall come to know Him better in His greatness and glory by taking a glimpse into the world of angels. In His omnipotence and love, in His creative power, God called the angels into existence, for He did not wish to be alone. Created in His image of radiant beauty, purity, strength and majesty, they rejoice before their God and Maker. They reflect the glory of God as the morning stars and praise Him as the sons of God (Job 38:4-7).

The angels of God are bright and shining beings, emanating light and mirroring the glory of God. Often when angels appear visibly, people fall to the ground, overwhelmed by their radiance, grandeur and power. In the angels they encounter something of God's holiness.

Thus Daniel writes that when the archangel Gabriel came to him, he was frightened and fell prostrate, yes, that he was stunned and became unconscious (Daniel 8:16ff.). Such was the effect of the angel's appearance upon him. On another occasion when Gabriel appeared to him, Daniel trembled with fear and

57

fell to the ground face downward in a deep faint. His strength left him and he grew pale and weak with fright till the angel said, "Fear not, be strong," at which he was strengthened (Daniel 10:8-19).

The mother of Samson experienced the same when a man of God whose "countenance was like the countenance of the angel of God" came to her to announce the birth and special commission of her son. She related to her husband that he was very awesome to see (Judges 13:6ff.).

Angels of God — mighty beings at the throne, from whom intense light energy radiates, because God, the source of light, can have full sway in them. When one angelic prince, an angel with great authority, descends from heaven, the whole earth is lit up by his radiance (Revelation 18:1). Who can fathom their splendour! The glory and light emanating from a single angel surpass all imagination. The angels, the first beings to be created by God, mirror the nature of God. Because they maintained the intimate relationship of love and reverence to God and continued to be dependent upon Him, especially in the hour of trial when Lucifer revolted against God, streams of ardour and life continually flow forth from God into them. The infinite power and greatness of God is manifested in them. In contrast to Satan, whose power is fragmented as a result of his separation from God, they are fully invested with divine power. Thus when an angel appeared and spoke to John on the island of Patmos, John not only fell down but wanted to worship him (Revelation 22:8).

Yes, the angels come directly from the realms of glory surrounding the throne of God. No man has ever seen God; but to the pure and sinless angels He reveals His countenance. These mighty warriors, who are endowed with divine strength to an inconceivable degree, reflect the glory of God in all its force and fullness. Occasionally, their appearance resembles that of our Lord Jesus, according to the descriptions of Daniel and John.

Daniel writes, "As I was standing on the bank of the great river, that is, the Tigris, I lifted up my eyes and looked, and behold, a man clothed in linen, whose loins were girded with gold of Uphaz. His body was like beryl, his face like the appearance of lightning, his eyes like flaming torches, his arms and legs like the gleam of burnished bronze, and the sound of his words like the noise of a multitude" (Daniel 10:4-6). And John saw "another mighty angel coming down from heaven, wrapped in a cloud, with a rainbow over his head, and his face was like the sun, and his legs like pillars of fire. He...called out with a loud voice, like a lion roaring; when he called out, the seven thunders sounded" (Revelation 10:1-3). This brings to mind the description of Jesus' appearance, whose eyes were like a flame of fire, whose feet were like burnished bronze, and whose voice was like the sound of many waters (Revelation 1:13-15).

With their majesty, power and beauty all these angelic beings proclaim the glory of the Lord, who created 'them. Their radiance comes from Jesus, through whom everything in heaven was created and who will one day illumine the New Jerusalem and the entire universe when the City of God descends upon the earth.

The inconceivable power and might that the angels possess in contrast to us wretched human beings also originate in Him who created and sustains the whole universe in His omnipotence. Likewise, their graceful bearing and beauty come from their Maker, the "fairest of the sons of men". Everything about them magnifies the beauty, glory, majesty and omnipotence of God.

Yes, in His angels, myriads upon myriads of them standing before Him, God sees the reflection of His greatness, power and glory, which they show forth in manifold ways. As a created being, each angel is an original, an individual, with distinctive characteristics and his own name. Every angel demonstrates a different aspect of God's glory, for in his uniqueness he reflects a specific attribute of God to the highest extent possible for a created being. Does this not fill us with adoration for the glory of God, seeing how imperfectly we reflect the image of God because of our sins?

By their very diversity and radiance the angelic hosts proclaim the manifold glories of God's nature. At the same time they show that it is impossible to plumb the depths of God's nature. A mere reflection in the angels – however glorious – does not do justice, for His greatness cannot be measured; the fullness of life proceeding from Him is boundless; and His glory surpasses all comprehension. When thinking about the angels, who would not feel constrained to worship the Triune God? They declare what God is like. By observing the nature of the angels, their missions in heaven and on earth, and their authority, we are given a new and deeper insight into God's nature – more so than by merely contemplating all that He has created on earth. God lives in the angels, as He made known to Moses: "Never defy him [the angel]...since I am manifest in him" (Exodus 23:21 MOFFATT). God is the God of the angels, for that is His name – the Lord of Sabaoth, the Lord of hosts. If we do not recognize God in His angels, we have an incomplete picture of Him, for as His name implies God is inseparable from His angels. He is always surrounded by them. This is evident at His throne, where they offer praise and adoration as their great and primary commission.

5
The Angels' Ministry of Adoration

The royal throne of the almighty Triune God in His heavenly kingdom is surrounded by the angelic hosts. Closest to God's throne are the cherubim and the seraphim, followed by thrones, dominions, principalities, powers, virtues, archangels, angels. In this order the nine choirs of angels defined by Church tradition praise God.

The four living creatures, the cherubim, constantly encircle the throne. Primordial beings manifesting the power of God, they guard the throne just as Scripture describes them guarding the entrance to paradise with a flaming sword indicative of flashes of lightning. The cherubim are the throne-bearers: "the God of Israel...enthroned above the cherubim" (2 Kings 19:15). They are the chariot carrying the throne of God, as Ezekiel saw in his vision: "Now the glory of the God of Israel had gone up from the cherubim on which it rested" (Ezekiel 9:3).

Thus the cherubim are in the immediate presence of God, partly constituting His throne and possessing inconceivable power. They are capable of bearing the almighty, eternal God, for the Creator God "rode on a cherub, and flew; he came swiftly upon the wings of the wind" (Psalm 18:10). Without the cherubim the throne of God and His glory would be incomplete, for the cherubim are an integral part of them. In the Holy of Holies where God dwelt and sat enthroned, representations of the cherubim were to be found on the Ark of the Covenant. Endowed with dynamic power and untold force, the cherubim surround the throne like quivering flames and mountains of blazing fire.

Above the throne of God are the seraphim, the angels of love, who do not have a corporality in the earthly sense but celestial bodies unrestricted by space and time. Veiled in awe and reverence, they stand before God in His holiness, covering their faces and feet with their wings. Their standing is best described as hovering, for they fly as shining, flashing angelic beings, in whom the consuming fire has the appearance of a streaming flame.

In the movements of the seraphim a mighty anthem of praise can be heard. Absorbed by the greatness and holiness of God, they extol Him and proclaim who He is, calling to one another, "Holy, holy, holy is the Lord of hosts; the whole earth is full of his glory" (Isaiah 6:2f.). So powerful is their worship that the Temple is filled with smoke and the foundations of its thresholds shake. The words used by Isaiah in describing this awesome scene of adoration are suggestive of an earthquake. The thundering praises lifted up to the holy God are attended by mighty tremors.

God is surrounded by these majestic, celestial messengers, figures of living, flowing light and splendour, beauty and power. At the same time He is hidden from the sight of man, being enveloped as if in a cloud by the seraphim and other angels. The adoration rises like smoke from flames of fire. By their very appearance the angelic hosts show forth what God is like — a consuming fire, whom none can approach. "God is clothed with terrible majesty" (Job 37:22), for the exalted angelic princes surrounding Him are like brilliant streaks of lightning.

The Revelation of John portrays a heavenly worship service held in the presence of God, the Maker, and the Lamb of God (Revelation 4 and 5). Seated upon the throne in transcendent brightness is the great and mighty One, surrounded by the twenty-four elders, who are arrayed in white garments, with crowns of gold upon their heads.

Around the throne we see again the four living creatures, who with their mighty cherub wings are the most glorious of all God's created beings. They combine all the perfections of created life. They are prototypes of creation who, dwelling in the presence of God, receive the most perfect revelation of Him. The eternal God, their Maker, who is the very essence of life and bears within Him the fullness of never-ending life, has made them partakers of this abundance of life. Thus in the four living creatures the perfection of God's creation is represented at the throne and worships God, while a mighty host of thousands upon thousands of angels proclaims the fullness of divine life and glorifies Him.

Multitudes of angels, myriads upon myriads of them, worship at the throne on high. Among them are the "seven angels who stand before God" (Revelation 8:2), commonly thought to be the seven archangels. Holy Scripture mentions the archangel Michael, who is one of the chief princes in the realm of the angels (Daniel 10:13) and who has been placed in charge of the people of God (Daniel 12:1). Reference is also made to Gabriel (Daniel 8:16; Luke 1:19) and Raphael (Tobit 3:17).

When praise and adoration are offered before the throne, the angels are like the strings of an instrument on which God Himself plays and from which He evokes the most glorious sounds, songs of adoration and melodies of exquisite beauty, combining gentleness and power and transcending all human imagination. Anthem upon anthem is raised by the angels to the Lamb that was slain and that procured salvation for mankind and the world by His death. Myriads upon myriads of angels pay homage to the Lamb, jubilantly praising Jesus, the pure and holy One, the Son of God. Shining like the stars, these light-emanating beings encircle Jesus in His royal splendour and glory. Amid blissful rejoicing their song, "Glory to the Lamb!" resounds throughout the heavens. The steps leading up to the throne vibrate at the thrice-repeated "Holy, holy, holy, Father, Son and Spirit!" And radiant like the sun, the Lamb stands in regal splendour at the throne with a gleaming crown upon His head. All about Him is brilliant light. But brighter than the glowing fire at the throne are the holy wounds of Jesus, by which He wrought eternal salvation.

Then, as if pointing prophetically to the consummation of God's eternal counsels, the scene of adoration takes on greater dimensions. Strains of the heavenly anthems at the throne are wafted down to earth, where people are listening from afar. At the sound of Jesus' name, the Lamb of God, a sweetness fills their hearts and they are drawn into the jubilation and worship. The heavens, the earth and everything beneath it tremble in bliss at the sound of the glorious anthems raised in honour of the Triune God, and in the end the whole universe joins in worshipping the Lamb (Revelation 5:13).

The adoration of the angels in heaven, at the throne of God, is of such dynamic force that it em-

65

braces the entire cosmos, causing one and all to join in till a magnificent choir is formed of billions of created beings, angels, humans and creatures prostrating themselves before the throne. Great and small, they all wish to offer praise to the Lamb. Expressing their love and gratitude, they bow down before Him and worship the Father, Son and Spirit. Yes, all creation, all living beings in heaven and on earth, beneath the earth, and even in the sea, blend their voices in a symphony of praise and adoration. Their one desire is to spend themselves ministering to the Lord, glorifying God and the Lamb, and giving thanks for His sacrifice, which brought redemption to the world.

Only the rushing sound of jubilant hymns of praise can be heard at the throne of God. In divine majesty Jesus, the Lamb of God, shines forth with an ever-increasing radiance, while the multitudes before the throne fall down in reverence, filled with awe at the sight of His wounds. One and all have united in glorifying the Lamb of God and giving Him ceaseless praise. Once it was only the angels who continually drank in His features, deriving full satisfaction from beholding His likeness. Now every living being in the cosmos is enthralled by the sight of the Lamb and this manifestation of the outpouring, sacrificial love of God.

This vision of a heavenly worship service before the throne shows us what it will be like one day when, at the end of the apocalyptic age, Satan is bound.

The angels were the first to rejoice before God when as the morning stars and sons of God they sang praises unto Him (Job 38:7). And today it is the angels who seek to inspire us to do the same — we who have been ransomed by the Lamb of God to be kings and priests at His throne. They long to see us gazing at Him to our hearts' content as they do and praising Jesus ardently. The angelic world is waiting for the unique adoration of the ransomed, who unlike the pure and sinless angels were once enslaved by sin and would have been lost for ever in blackest darkness if Jesus, the Lamb of God, had not purchased them with His precious blood.

Offering up praise and worship — what a great and very wonderful ministry has been entrusted to the angels! And the day is coming when all living beings will take part in this liturgy, in this ministry of adoration. In Hebrews 1:14 it says, "Are they [the angels] not all ministering [literally: liturgical] spirits?" — in other words, worshipping spirits.

Fire from God's throne seems to have entered their very beings. Filled with ardour, they feel constrained to encircle the throne without pause, praising the Triune God for who He is. It is as if they had absorbed the sublimity, majesty, omnipotence and glory of God and, having done so, are consumed with the desire to reveal to everyone the Lord enthroned and reigning. The throne is lifted up, as it were, by angelic hands for all the world to behold God in His glory while angelic tongues proclaim unceasingly, "Who is like the Lord our God, the Maker and Ruler of all worlds!"

Together the angelic princes and choirs of angels make known to mankind the glory and greatness of God in His kingdom. Lifting the veil from our mortal eyes, they allow us a glimpse of the vastness and omnipotence of God as they proclaim the glories of God and worship Him. In sharing these mysteries with us, they wish to draw us into this adoration of God.

By their very nature and aura the angels give us an

inkling of what God is like and how we should approach Him. They show us that we can come to know Him more deeply by offering up praise and adoration that are centred on Him alone. This kind of praise is a powerful form of worship, a jubilant anthem in honour of God, because it originates from total dedication to God. The angels seek only God's approval. They are centred on Him alone, having no personal wish or request. "God alone" is their motto. In Him they find complete satisfaction. They circle around Him like a planet orbiting its sun. They are completely absorbed in God and delight in gazing upon His image, which they are privileged to behold. As for us human beings, in the life to come only the pure in heart, that is, only those who are sanctified, will be allowed to behold Him in fulfilment of their deepest longings.

6
The Authority Granted to the Angels

Now and then, as we have seen, the Lord lifts the veil slightly and reveals something of the heavenly world, the real world, where the angels have their specific tasks. Just as John was shown a worship service in heaven, God permitted Daniel to see the divine court in session: "Thrones were placed [for the assessors with the Judge], and the Ancient of days [God, the eternal Father] took His seat, Whose garment was white as snow, and the hair of His head like pure wool; His throne was like the fiery flame, its wheels were burning fire. A stream of fire came forth from before Him; a thousand thousands ministered to Him, and ten thousand times ten thousand rose up and stood before Him; the Judge was seated — the court was in session — and the books were opened" (Daniel 7:9f. AB).

Seated upon the highest throne as the Sovereign of all worlds, God manifests Himself as Judge of all worlds, before whom every person is exposed and before whose eyes nothing that we have done is concealed, whether good or evil. God manifests Himself — He whose judgment none can escape and before whose judgment seat everyone must appear one day to receive the recompense for what he has done during his earthly life, all of which has been recorded in the books.

"Holy, holy, holy is the Lord God of hosts!" We

can almost see these words written over His throne, which is like a fiery flame and from which a stream of fire proceeds, declaring that God is a consuming fire.

At this court of the thrice holy God, where the eternal destiny of people, nations and the world is determined, the Son of God is presented — He who has been given power, honour, glory, and dominion over all worlds (Daniel 7:13f.). All the first-created sons of God, the angels, take part in this session. The Lord of Sabaoth, the God of the heavenly hosts, does nothing without them. Whenever God the Father or Jesus Christ appear in glory and sublime power as Ruler of all worlds to pronounce judgment upon the earth, causing it to shake and tremble, the angels are also present. They accompany God like a cloud in which He manifests or conceals Himself.

The honour that God has bestowed upon the angels is inconceivable. They are permitted to be in His presence continually, whereas people who are not pure in heart will be hurled away. The angels are like the hem or train of God's garment, inseparable from Him. Their eyes are ever directed towards His countenance, even when their duties call them elsewhere. They do not detach themselves from God, who is the very source of life for them. What a contrast to us human beings, who usually lead a life detached from God! Even as believers we find nothing so hard as abiding in Him. Yes, the angels are permitted to be with God the Father and Jesus always. What a blessed privilege that must be for the angels! Being very close to God and living in His presence, they are endued with great power, participating in His mighty, judicial acts and in the realization of His eternal plans and purposes.

What a tremendous occasion it will be in divine

history when Jesus appears in glory! And when that moment comes, He will be revealed to the world not on His own but with His angels (Matthew 25:31). Then He will sit on the throne of His glory, and all the nations will be gathered before Him and He will separate the people as a shepherd separates the sheep from the goats (Matthew 25:32). Once again the divine court will be in session, and once again the angels will be present, just as the Lord showed Daniel.

In addition to the judgment of the world in general, Jesus speaks of the judgment awaiting His disciples. When referring to this, he stresses the importance of following Him in truth and keeping His commandments. He tells them that when He comes in the glory of His Father He will reward everyone according to his deeds (Matthew 16:27). This brings to mind the words of the apostle Paul that we must all appear before the judgment seat of Christ, so that each one may be repaid for what he has done during his life, whether good or evil (2 Corinthians 5:10).

On that day when Jesus comes to recompense His followers, He will not come on His own. Rather, He will "come with his angels in the glory of his Father". The angels will be present when the books are opened, for they attended us throughout our earthly lives, following our plans, struggles and work. They watched over our souls as well as our bodies. They played a significant role in our combat with the powers of darkness, helping us on to victory. They fought on our behalf against the demons, who sought to ensnare us. Yes, they will have a say in the court proceedings, as in the case of the high priest Joshua, who according to the accusations of Satan should have incurred judgment. However, the angel of the Lord spoke on his behalf and thus he was spared and pardoned (Zechariah 3:1-5).

The positions of honour that God has given the angels and the power with which He has invested them are so great that they are hardly conceivable to sinful man's limited understanding. But in His Word God gives us an indication of the angels' might, so that we who are sorely pressed and tempted by Satan and his demons, can see what wonderful guardians and warriors He has sent out to minister to us. Because Satan is constantly about us as a roaring lion, these mighty warriors surround us every minute of our lives, sustaining us. With His references to the close relationship between the angels and the Father and Himself, Jesus seeks to imprint the truth upon our hearts: God and the angels belong together.

Speaking of the diabolical world, do we not also associate the demons with Satan? Indeed, we cannot imagine the demons apart from Satan. As the opponent of Jesus Christ, Satan is merely imitating the close relationship between Jesus and His angels. Just as Jesus has a whole army of angels who appear with Him and battle at His side and who are involved and empowered in the executive administration of His divine strategy, so Satan has gathered around him the host of fallen angels, who joined in his revolt and now assist in implementing his plans as his demon troops.

Satan and his demons form a diabolical unity as a counterfeit of the unity formed by Jesus and His holy angels. For the apostles, it was a matter of course that God and the angels belong together. Paul, for instance, says in reference to the return of Jesus, "...when the Lord Jesus is revealed from heaven with his mighty angels in flaming fire" (2 Thessalonians 1:7). Jesus Himself shows the angels great honour, saying, for example, "Every one who acknowledges me before men, the Son of man also will acknowledge before the angels of God; but he who denies me before men will be denied before the angels of God" (Luke 12:8f.).

With that, Jesus points out the great importance of a person being acknowledged by Him as His disciple in the presence of the angels. What a high regard God must have for the angels! Indeed, what honour Jesus shows the angels when He says, "He who conquers...I will not blot his name out of the book of life; I will confess his name before my Father and before his angels" (Revelation 3:5).

Here the angels are mentioned in the same breath as the Father. What an incomparable honour for a person to be acknowledged by Jesus Christ in the presence of the Father as one whose name is written in the book of life and whose place is at His side in the realms of heavenly glory! And this important declaration is made by Jesus in the presence of not only the Father but the angels — an indication of the value Jesus sets on the angels and of their exalted position in the celestial world. Indeed, the angels have the great honour of always beholding the countenance of God. Few human beings are granted this sublime privilege, for without sanctification no one will behold the Lord (Hebrews 12:14).

Just how highly Jesus regards this privilege of the angels and honours them for it, is evident from His word, "Never despise one of these little ones; I tell you, they have their guardian angels in heaven, who look continually on the face of my heavenly Father" (Matthew 18:10 NEB). The fact that these little ones are in the care of angels who always see the face of God is so tremendous and overwhelming that no one should look down on them.

The disciples and apostles of Jesus also held the angels in high regard. In his first letter to Timothy, Paul writes, "I charge you before God and the Lord Jesus Christ and the elect angels that you observe these things" (1 Timothy 5:21 RAV). Again, God the Father and our Lord Jesus Christ are mentioned in the same breath as the elect angels. What honour Paul shows the angels here!

That we are so little conscious of the mighty position of the angels is surely a great loss to our spiritual lives. For instance, when counselling a person, we might well admonish him before God and Jesus Christ but never before His holy angels. Today we have forgotten what an elevated position the angels have before God and what authority they are granted over us human beings. We no longer treat the angels with respect, nor do we have a wholesome fear of demons. Both attitudes expose us more to the attacks of demons and cause us much harm and suffering. What a source of strength it would be for us to know that the holy armies of heaven, those mighty warriors, the angels, are battling on behalf of us weak mortals! But we lack this knowledge. If, however, we do not appreciate the angels as Jesus does, we are no longer standing on Holy Scripture, and that always has grave consequences for our spiritual lives.

Moreover, in so doing we grieve and dishonour the almighty God, who is both our Father and Judge and who calls Himself the Lord of Sabaoth, the Lord of hosts; and we dishonour Jesus, who has revealed to us how close the angels are to Him. Whoever loves Jesus also loves those who belong to Him and whom He loves and honours. The angels, the first of His created beings, are far superior to us human beings (2 Peter 2:11). Ever since the Fall man's insight and intellect have been impaired. But the power and discernment of the angels are intact. They also possess great authority in the universe with vast spheres of influence assigned to them. They are involved in the far-reaching plans of God. They are allowed to help carry out His divine purposes, even in connection with His redemptive work for mankind.

The insight that the angels are given into God's plans and the extent to which they rule with God are scarcely comprehensible to us human beings. In Matthew 24:36 Jesus says, "But of that day and hour no one knows, not even the angels of heaven, nor the Son, but the Father only." This seems to imply that all the other plans are known to the Son. At the same time this scripture makes an astonishing reference to the power of the angels and their position of honour with God. From this verse we may infer that, like the Son, the angels are given an insight into the great, divine counsels of God. Confirming this is the fact that angels were always heralds of momentous occasions in divine history or were actively involved in them as, for instance, during the divine revelation on Mount Sinai.

When God manifested Himself at Sinai in His holiness and majesty, it was as if His throne had come down. "Mount Sinai was wrapped in smoke, for the Lord descended upon it in fire; its smoke ascended like that of a furnace, and the whole mountain quaked greatly" (Exodus 19:18 AB). This is similar to the description of His throne in heaven. There God is surrounded by His angels in blazing fire and glory, and so it was on the holy mountain of divine revelation. Holy Scripture refers to this event, saying, "The chariots of God are twenty thousand, even thousands of angels: the Lord is among them, as in Sinai, in the holy place" (Psalm 68:17 AV). In Deuteronomy 33:2 the following account is given: "The Lord came to us at Mount Sinai, and dawned upon us from Mount Seir; he shone from Mount Paran, surrounded by ten thousands of holy angels, and with flaming fire at his right hand" (LB).

Thus the angels were more than witnesses of that awe-inspiring moment when the eternal God made a covenant with sinful human beings – with His chosen people Israel, from whom the Saviour of the world was to come – and when He gave them, as the expression of His will, the Ten Commandments, the basis of all law and order in human life. The angels were actively involved in this mighty event, for as Stephen said, "you who received the Law that angels transmitted" (Acts 7:53 MOFFATT). Elsewhere it says, "The message [Law] given to our ancestors by the angels was shown to be true" (Hebrews 2:2 GNB). In another passage we read, "The Law was handed down by angels, with a man [Moses] acting as a go-between" (Galatians 3:19 GNB).

The magnitude of the angels' commission on that momentous occasion in divine and world history is almost inconceivable. Through their agency the mighty revelation of the will of God, as expressed in the Ten Commandments, was given to man. Nor was that event on Mount Sinai the only time when angels were present. Whenever something decisive occurred in God's divine plans and purposes, the angels were also on the scene, as implied by Jesus' words about their association with Him and the Father.

When the fullness of time came and the Saviour was to enter the world, angels were once again involved. God chose them as His holy messengers for this most significant event in human and divine his-

76

tory. This is yet another indication that the angels are given insight into the plans of God and His eternal purposes concerning the world, mankind, His chosen people, the body of believers, and the nations. Nonetheless, the angels, who are created beings, cannot fully comprehend their Creator God and His thoughts. The only one who can is God Himself.

If the angels played such an active role at the making of the covenant and the giving of the Ten Commandments, how much more so on this momentous occasion in divine history! This event involved *their* Lord, through whom they were created and whom they were now to worship as He was about to enter the world as the First-born (Hebrews 1:6). The moment had come for Him to leave heaven in order to be made "for a little while lower than the angels" (Hebrews 2:7 GNB) and become a human being. He would be delivered into the hands of men and then nailed to the cross amid untold suffering, shame and disgrace. What immeasurable grief all this meant for the angels, for was not Jesus the radiant Sun of heaven, around whom they revolved?

It is impossible to describe what must have been going on in the heart of the archangel Gabriel when he was commissioned to deliver this message to Mary and thus proclaim the irrevocable decision: Jesus would come to earth in order to begin His path of sorrows to the cross. Now it was going to happen – an event that must have filled the angels' hearts with deepest grief coupled with inexpressible adoration. They probably found it hard to grasp that God so loved the world that He gave His only begotten Son, even allowing Him to die, in order to redeem man enslaved by sin.

Thus the archangel Gabriel is given a part in that

key event in divine history when God's act of salvation for mankind was to begin. He knew about the miracle of the virgin birth, that the Holy Spirit would come upon Mary and that the power of the Most High would overshadow her. He was the one who brought Mary these tremendous tidings. He knew that the Holy One to be born of her was the Son of God, who would one day sit upon the throne of David.

Furthermore, the angel Gabriel knew that by a mighty act of God Elizabeth had conceived a son in her old age. He was aware of the individual phases of God's saving work in connection with Jesus — namely, that someone would first come to prepare the way for Him. And that man was John. Thus he announced to Zacharias that John would prepare a people for the Lord and go before Him in the spirit and power of Elijah, to turn back the hearts of the fathers to the children.

Likewise, an angel having knowledge of God's plan of salvation appeared to Joseph in a dream before the birth of Jesus and announced the coming of the Messiah, who was to be called Jesus, for "he will save his people from their sins" (Matthew 1:20f.). And in that great and unique hour when Jesus, the incarnate Word, was born as a Babe and lay in a manger in Bethlehem, it was the angels who declared the incredible yet true and joyful tidings to the shepherds, "Unto you is born this day in the city of David a Saviour" (Luke 2:9-14 AV). Again, when it became necessary to protect the new-born Saviour and Redeemer of mankind from the fury of Herod, an angel of the Lord appeared to Joseph in a dream and gave the command to flee to Egypt, later calling him back to Israel (Matthew 2:13,19f.).

At every strategic point in divine history we see the involvement of God's angels. Whether at Mount Sinai, at the birth of Jesus, at His temptation in the wilderness and later in Gethsemane, at His resurrection, ascension, return in glory or during the judgments in the era of wrath prior to His return — whenever something tremendous occurs in the unfolding of God's purposes, angels are present too, assisting God.

Thus the archangel Gabriel, who may be especially commissioned for key events in divine history, made known to Daniel God's plan for the end times. Another angel, or so we may assume, called to Gabriel, saying, "Tell this man the meaning of the vision" (Daniel 8:16 NIV). "As he [Gabriel] came near the place where I was standing, I was terrified and fell prostrate. 'Son of man,' he said to me...'I am going to tell you what will happen later in the time of wrath, because the vision concerns the appointed time of the end.'"(Daniel 8:17,19 NIV).

The insight God has given the angels reaches even to the end of time. He has endowed them with a large portion of His wisdom, understanding and power, granting them extensive knowledge of His inscrutable thoughts and designs. Yes, God has given the angels insight into what is really going on, revealing to them His hand in everything that happens. They can see how, step by step, God is leading the history of mankind and of the nations according to His plan.

Angels of God! — Who can comprehend what a position of honour they have before the almighty God? Who can grasp what power they possess? In this day and age when we are greatly imperilled by satanic forces God wants us to know what mighty warriors are battling on our behalf, so that we shall

79

come to appreciate and experience their power as never before.

7
Angelic Activity
in the Universe and Nations

The centre of the angelic ministry of adoration is the throne of God. The bowing and prostration at the divine throne, the flames of fire, the coming and going of celestial messengers, and what we hear from their reports — all speak of a kingdom in which the angels live as co-regents and co-workers of God. They form a perfect angelic state, a well-ordered hierarchy. At the highest level are the exalted angelic princes, those mighty angels at the throne, known as the cherubim and seraphim. We may assume that the throne council is made up of a small group of angels to whom Lucifer may also have belonged in the beginning, perhaps even once fulfilling this function on his own. Beneath them are the thrones and dominions, principalities, powers and virtues, whereas the wide base of the pyramid is composed of the archangels and the vast multitudes of angels, who are sent out to minister to us. Great power and authority has been bestowed upon these mighty and glorious angels.

From the allusions made in Holy Scripture we may infer that God has divided the vast territory of His kingdom into provinces, which He has entrusted to exalted angelic princes as their domains and areas of administration.[9] It is commonly held that Lucifer received the earth as his domain. At the temptation of our Lord in the wilderness, Satan showed Him all the kingdoms of the world in a moment of time and said, "All this authority I will give you, and their glory; for this has been delivered to me, and I give it to whoever I wish" (Luke 4:5f. RAV). According to many theologians the magnificent celestial bodies — the stars — are also the domains of angels.[10]

God has entrusted the angels with great and mighty commissions in His kingdom, and this goes especially for the angelic princes. In this heavenly kingdom they have been appointed as God's representatives.

Very likely, there is a connection between the angelic world and the laws of nature, or the natural forces.

When we look at the celestial bodies in the sky, we ask who determines their course. When we look upon the earth and consider the marvellous growth of its vegetation, we ask who is the motivating force. How pertinent such questions are; yet how seldom they are posed...The laws of nature, which are scientifically verified, can not of their own accord bring things into existence. They require other forces working in conjunction with them. Science is concerned with the study of the laws of nature. But why the forces of nature work and what sets them in motion science can not explain. It is Holy Scripture that makes such things known to us. Therefore, it is not necessary to assume that science and Holy Scripture are mutually exclusive. The Pool of Bethesda had healing properties when the water was stirred up from time to time. Holy Scripture tells us that an angel was responsible (John 5:4)...Sodom and Gomorrah were destroyed by volcanic eruptions and lava flow. Holy Scripture refers to the involvement of angels (Genesis 19:13).[11]

Even though Holy Scripture does not always mention angelic presence in such incidents and even though we know that both protection and judgment ultimately come from God, it is evident from the witness of the Bible that God employs angels to carry out His plans, designating them as co-workers and investing them with great power.

In Revelation, John sees an angel who appears to be in charge of the waters (Revelation 16:5) and another angel who has power over fire (Revelation 14:18). In Revelation 7:1 we hear of four angels standing at the four corners of the earth and protecting the world from perilous, destructive winds.

What is the meaning of all this? The course of the stars, the growth of plants, the forces of nature and the protection we experience — all positive occurrences in living creation somehow have a connection with the dealings of God and angelic activity. This is in accordance with God's holy order. In the processes of growth and decay in our changing world, the angels act as sentries at the boundaries appointed by God. They are His executive administrators, in charge of creatures and forces that God has brought into existence.[12]

Yes, God has put the angels in charge of nature, the visible creation. They have been given power over the elements and presumably over material substances. The entire creation is inseparable from angelic activity. To them has been given the administration of all creation.[13]

In comparison with the angels, whose power and authority extend to all of God's creation and the entire universe, man with his small and limited power and authority on planet earth is a mere nothing. The tremendous power of the angels gives us an idea of the immeasurable power of the Maker, who created all these angelic princes and put them in charge of such large administrative domains.

What vast spheres of influence have been entrusted to the angelic princes when we consider, for instance, the galaxies! This involves dimensions beyond the scope of the human mind. Many millions of miles separate the earth from the other planets, and many billions of miles lie between us and other solar systems. As someone once phrased it:

Now I see that all the stars that were ever observed in the skies, all the millions of shining dots making up the Milky Way, the innumerable celestial bodies, suns of varying sizes and brightness, solar systems, planets, asteroids, millions and billions of them moving in the space that surrounds us: that which we call with our human tongues "the universe" is in comparison to the never-ending outer space nothing more than a group of celestial islands or a city in a vast and densely populated country.[14]

All this lies within the angelic sphere of influence, but so too, presumably, the elements known to us, such as fire and water. Angels appear to be stationed everywhere, exercising control over celestial bodies, the waters and the elements. How reassuring this is! They battle against the demons, the fallen angels, who seek to use everything in creation for destructive purposes.

"The heavens declare the glory of God" (Psalm

19:1 NIV). Yes, the heavenly realm, the realm of the angels, where the Almighty reigns, giving them commands concerning the administration of the entire creation, tells us what God is like in His omnipotence. It tells us about the throne of God, exalted above all worlds. From there the perfect rule of God goes forth into all the universe. No human being is capable of fathoming the deep and mighty counsels of God. How great and awe-inspiring, therefore, are the commissions of the angels, their duties and ranks, and how immeasurably great their domains, which are beyond the scope of the human eye and mind because they embrace the cosmos!

How deeply comforting is the knowledge that in the end times when the elements such as fire, water and nuclear energy are let loose, it is the angels who have control of these forces! When through the agency of His angels the Lord unleashes the elements, turning them into destructive forces, His own will experience miracles. The angels will command the elements not to cause any harm to those who truly love and fear God.

The greatness of God is further demonstrated by other forms of authority granted to the angels, for God has appointed them as watchers to oversee the course of events in world history. Throughout the reaches of space and the ages of time the angels of God operate behind the scenes in the complex course of history. They watch over the body of believers and supervise the affairs of mankind. These mighty ones and executives of the divine will (Psalm 103:20f.) provide protection, execute judgment, battle against demonic forces and guide man. In the Book of Daniel a report is given of a decree made by a council of angels and then proclaimed with a loud voice by one of the holy watchers: a verdict upon King Nebuchadnezzar. "The sentence is by the decree of the watchers, the decision by the word of the holy ones, to the end that the living may know that the Most High rules the kingdom of men" (Daniel 4:17).

Here we see the intervention of angelic princes in world history. Through a decree made by the council of angels Nebuchadnezzar, the world ruler of those days, was deposed and his kingdom was taken away from him. An event that shocked the whole world at the time and went down in the annals of history.

These watchers seem to exert considerable influence on world politics, even if they do not govern everything in the minutest detail. Their task is to prevent man from overstepping the ultimate holy boundaries appointed by God and to withstand the demonic forces.

At the same time these angels are executors of God's judgments. On account of their extensive authority, the life of the nations is affected by their decrees and orders, and what they say comes to pass. Nonetheless, their power to command is nothing compared with the omnipotence of God, who is the supreme Ruler of all worlds.

Do our hearts not rejoice to think of the Lord's promise that when we are small and insignificant we have an angel beside us, for then we belong to those "little ones" He speaks of in the Gospels. We have seen what power and influence the angels have, even being able to decree the death of a person or to command the elements, yes, to oppose and conquer the demons.

They were engaged in warfare with the demon powers long before the end times. We read, for instance, that on his way to Daniel, the angel Gabriel was withstood by the fallen angelic prince or demon in charge of Persia, and a conflict ensued. Later he had to face the fallen angelic prince of Greece (Daniel 10:13,20).

From these incidents we see that not only do Satan and his demons operate behind the scenes in our personal lives and activities, but their negative influence can also be felt in the life of the nations. The angels, both fallen and unfallen, are actively involved in what happens on earth. The earthly battles are first fought out in the spirit realm (Ephesians 3:10; 6:12; Revelation 12:7).

Great and beneficent spirit beings have been commanded to work in the nations of the world towards the realization of God's eternal plans and purposes. Also at work are demonic vassals of Satan, ambassadors of the prince of darkness. Hostile to God, these evil spirits are determined to destroy the standards that God has given in His commandments for the moral well-being of the nations, and are bent on leading the nations into ruin. They want to create chaos — a satanic, demonic chaos, instigated by the devil. They want to entice a nation to blatant self-worship and consummate pride — hubris. Thus they battle against the holy angelic prince who has been placed in charge of that particular nation and who acts as a frontier-guard of its moral code. For instance, the angelic prince Michael battles on behalf of God's people Israel. From the Book of Daniel we learn that the angelic princes support one another on the basis of their alliance (Daniel 10:13,21).

Again, we are given a glimpse of angels acting as representatives of God in world events. Mighty angelic princes are appointed to individual nations as guardian angels, watchers, warners, administrators of judgment and punishment. The destiny of the nations is fought out in the unseen world, where demonic powers and principalities war with the holy angelic princes. Who can say how much trouble, effort, toil and warfare it must cost the angels to carry out their function as guardians of the nations and individuals entrusted to their care?

Protecting, judging, battling, supervising — every service rendered by these thousands of angels to nations, individuals and the kingdom of God, however awe-inspiring, pales in comparison with the dealings of God. The ministry of angels is but a dim reflection of the way God watches over everything and how His heart throbs with love and sorrow for us, the nations and His creation in the fervent desire to help us. Words cannot adequately express how God calls and warns us, suffers and seeks to win us back and to what lengths He will go to accomplish His purposes concerning people, nations, the Body of Christ, yes, every individual person.

The activity of the angels, the extent of their authority, and their devoted service all proclaim, "Who is like God!" How He must love the sons of men to send to their aid and service His mighty ones from the heavenly hosts!

8
Angelic Power in the End Times

At no point in time will the power, authority, greatness and strength of the angels be so evident as at the close of the age when they will be employed in carrying out God's judgments of wrath. To be sure, down through the ages the angels have served as executors of God's judgments, often punishing the foes of God's elect when the latter were in danger. We read that the angel of God helped to hold back the Egyptian army from the departing Israelites, who passed safely through the Red Sea, whereas the Egyptians were drowned in the water (Exodus 14:19f.). On another occasion the angel of the Lord went forth and slew 185,000 men in the camp of the Assyrians (2 Kings 19:35; Isaiah 37:36).

However, we also read of angels executing judgment upon the people of God or upon one of His chosen ones like David, who saw the destroying angel sent to execute judgment on his sin (2 Samuel 24). After "destroying throughout all the territory of Israel", the angel stood with his sword drawn against Jerusalem (1 Chronicles 21).

In this incident we are given a glimpse of angelic power in judgment, which in the end times will be displayed on a worldwide scale. Whatever is in the heart of God — saving love or anguished wrath — is imparted to His angels, who are utterly devoted to Him, serving Him in rapt attention, ever ready to carry out

His commands. They are transmitters in the truest sense of the word, transmitting His nature, His will, His thoughts and His words.

That which is in God can also be found in their hearts, thoughts and speech. At the close of the age this will become overwhelmingly evident when the anguished wrath of God, having been restrained for so long, will be poured out upon an utterly depraved humanity that ruined the earth He created and turned it into hell. Thus the wrath of God will descend in reaction, or rather, as a counteraction, to the horrors of sin.

During this period the fury of Satan and his demons reaches a peak. They are driven from their domain in the air and thrown down to earth, while the demons of the bottomless pit emerge from their prison to come upon the earth. Like a mighty army, vast numbers of demons patrol the earth under the direction of the master strategist, Satan, to win for themselves people of every age, class and walk of life. The demonic spirits of impurity, lust, rebellion, lying, and sorcery advance further and further.

Then begins the counter-attack. The hour of divine judgment draws near when the angelic hosts, the armies of God, come forward in the power of God so as to crush the large-scale attack of Satan and his endeavour to satanize and demonize the world and humanity. Filled with ardour, those mighty warriors of God, the angels, prepare for their operations. Once again Michael enters into warfare with Satan and his demons, who have devastated the whole world. He is assisted not only by the angels in his choir but by the entire angelic hierarchy. From the highest to the lowest choir they form up in ranks as a united force, a celestial army.

Then it is as if the adoration before the throne of God were interrupted by a strange hush like the calm before the storm. Mighty trumpet blasts resembling war-cries and loud peals of thunder signal the preliminaries of battle, while jubilant shouts like the sound of many waters announce the approaching victory. All of heaven, as Revelation shows us, is in a state of activity. Waves of grief and wrath proceed from the throne of God and sweep across the ten thousand times ten thousand angels making up His army. They are seized with God's grief and wrath over His sin-ravaged world and over man who was created in God's image but now reflects the image of Satan.

A single glance or a word of command from God, the almighty Judge of the world, sends the heavenly spirits flying like arrows in all directions to execute His judgments upon the world and mankind. Charged with holy wrath, these mighty heroes of God enter the final conflict with Satan and battle on till the victory is accomplished.

The world-shaking hour of God's wrath, which marks a turning-point in world history, sees all of heaven in action, with angelic princes and angels carrying out the divine directives instantaneously. One wave of wrath follows the other. Out of the seal judgments come the trumpet judgments, to be followed by the bowls of wrath. For thousands of years God in His infinite patience and goodness virtually remained silent in the face of all the evil on earth. But now when the vats of evil overflow (Joel 3:13), He emerges from His silence. He speaks by taking action and in so doing shows that He is the living Lord and Judge. He begins to judge His world with the angels as His instruments. From His throne He gives His

91

angels the commands to execute judgment. And, behold, the whole earth trembles at His majesty and under His blows of judgment when the angels, in obedience to God's holy directives, step forth to pour out His holy wrath upon the earth.

Throughout the world one can almost sense the anguished wrath and suspense of the angels at every mighty trumpet blast. Shouting with a loud voice, like that of a roaring lion (Revelation 10:3), they seek to rouse the sinful world from its deathlike sleep. Yes, one can sense in them the lava flow of God's wrath because of this sinful Babylon of a world, for which the Son of God gave His life. With all his might an angel flings into the sea a boulder like a great millstone and in holy wrath announces the impending judgment: "Thus with violence the great city Babylon shall be thrown down, and shall not be found any more" (Revelation 18:21 RAV).

No man can fully comprehend what it means for the angels to witness this hour of God's wrath. They experienced the hour of trial for the angelic world — the revolt of Lucifer, his apostasy and fall. He had been one of them — their pride and glory, the most brilliant and most beautiful of all created beings in heaven. They also witnessed the creation of man and then his fall, which was instigated by Satan. They were placed with flaming sword at the entrance to paradise, from which man was expelled. For the sake of men, nations, yes, all creation they had to enter combat with the demons.

They witnessed, no doubt with immeasurable grief — otherwise there would not be such rejoicing among the angels of God when a sinner repents (Luke 15:10) — how Satan, the opponent and hater of God and mankind, claimed more and more victims down

92

through the ages. This they could not prevent, for God has given man freedom of will. No matter how much a guardian angel may battle and intervene for his charge, the ultimate decision for or against God rests with man.

With the dawning of the end times, the angels saw Satan furiously making an all-out effort to overpower and demonize large numbers of people and carry them off as his booty in the short span of time left to him. With what vigour, force and dynamic the angels, therefore, enter the end-time battle against Satan! It is an either-or situation: either the kingdom of Satan or the kingdom of God will win. Either the whole world will come under the dominion of Satan, whom men will worship in the form of the beast that rose out of the sea (Revelation 13); or else the world will come under the sole dominion of Jesus Christ. Now, when the cause of Jesus Christ is at stake more than ever before, the angels will prove that they really belong to Him and are on His side. This time of bitter conflict will also show what great power and authority the angels possess.

The seven angels who have their places before God — perhaps the archangels — stand ready to usher in the judgments. They are given seven trumpets and prepare to sound them (Revelation 8 and 9). Every trumpet blast is attended by a mighty event in accordance with the power granted to the angels in the end times.

When the first angel blows his trumpet, hail and fire, mingled with blood, descend upon the earth, and a third part of the earth is burnt, a third of the trees and every blade of green grass.

When the second angel blows his trumpet, something like a great mountain, burning with fire, is thrown into the sea. A third of the sea becomes blood, a third of the living creatures in the sea die, and a third of the ships are destroyed.

The third angel blows his trumpet and a great star falls from heaven, blazing like a torch, and poisoning a third of the rivers and springs of water, and many people die from drinking the water, which has become so bitter.

When the fourth mighty angel blows his trumpet, a third part of the sun is struck, a third of the moon, and a third of the stars, so that the third part of them turns dark, with a third of the light of the day and of the night failing.

When the fifth angel blows his trumpet, a star falls from the sky to the earth. The angel opens the shaft of the bottomless pit with the key given to him, and from the shaft rises smoke like the smoke of a vast furnace. Creatures resembling locusts emerge from the smoke and injure those human beings who do not bear the seal of God upon their foreheads.

The angels not only give the signal for the various judgments to begin, but they are also empowered to seal the servants of God (Revelation 7:3), so that the demonic forces (referred to as locusts) cannot harm them. Thus the power of the demons ascending from the bottomless pit is only partial. "They were commanded not to harm the grass of the earth, or any green thing, or any tree, but only those men who do not have the seal of God on their foreheads" (Revelation 9:4 RAV). And they must act accordingly. Without realizing it, they are instruments of God administering judgment to those people who do not bear the seal of God upon their foreheads but who belong to Satan. They are sent to torment them.

To His holy angels, however, God entrusts the actual judgments, those great and holy judgments upon the world. Another four angels, who have been held ready for the hour, the day, the month and the year, are released to kill a third of mankind (Revelation 9:14f.).

In addition to these angels of judgment the Book of Revelation shows us other angels involved in the end-time events: warners and heralds of judgment. The entire cosmos is, as it were, under the control of angels, who do all they can for the establishment of Jesus' reign. There is, for instance, the warning angel, who flies in midheaven (Revelation 14:6). The power he possesses is vast, and his missions are inconceivable to the human mind. He is commissioned to announce his message not just to one person, one city or one nation. No, this one angel has a message for all of mankind living in the end times. The everlasting gospel that he proclaims with a loud voice to the whole world simultaneously is, "Fear God and give him glory, for the hour of his judgment has come; and worship him who made heaven and earth, the sea and the fountains of water" (Revelation 14:7).

In former times we may well have wondered why this message is called an everlasting gospel. Today we no longer wonder why. In the spirit of the Antichrist, man in the end times revolts against everything associated with God and the worship of God, refusing to tolerate any authority above himself. This is his chief characteristic. The original relationship of the creature with its God and Maker, a relationship of awe and reverential fear, has been lost. And so the gospel proclaimed by the angel is a saving message for the end-time generation. Only when man humbles himself again before God, worships Him and gives Him glory, can he see himself as a sinner before God. And only then does he recognize his desperate need of a Saviour, Jesus.

Thus we see how certain angels are appointed to be warners for all mankind, proclaiming the message of God more forcefully and urgently than a human being ever could. Another warning angel cries with a loud voice, "If anyone worships the beast and his image, and receives his mark on his forehead or on his hand, he himself shall also drink of the wine of the wrath of God, which is poured out full strength into the cup of his indignation" (Revelation 14:9f. RAV).

Yet another angel announces the judgment: "Fallen, fallen is Babylon the great, she who made all nations drink the wine of her impure passion" (Revelation 14:8). Other angels with different but complementary functions in the task of executing judgment call to one another: "'Put in your sickle, and reap, for the hour to reap has come, for the harvest of the earth is fully ripe.' So he who sat upon the cloud swung his sickle on the earth, and the earth was reaped" (Revelation 14:15f.).

Not only have the angels been commissioned to proclaim judgment and execute it, but they have also been assigned to gather the condemned and deliver them into the kingdom of hell and, conversely, to escort the elect into heaven. Separating the good from the bad is part of their ministry among those living at the end of time. No doubt, the guardian angels have a special role in this task. "The Son of man will send his angels, and they will gather out of his kingdom all causes of sin and all evildoers, and throw them into the furnace of fire; there men will weep and gnash their teeth" (Matthew 13:41f.). On the other hand, Jesus will "send out his angels with a loud trumpet call" — an indication of how significant their ministry is — "and they will gather his elect from the four winds" (Matthew 24:31).

All these angels differ in their functions and power, as depicted by the symbols they carry. Some carry sickles; others carry bowls of wrath or a censer with incense mingled with the prayers of the saints; still others carry the trumpets, and so on (Revelation 8; 14; 16). They also come forth from different places. One angel, who has power over fire, comes forth from the altar. Another angel is seated on a cloud, and yet another comes out of the temple in heaven. And standing in the sun is a fourth angel. He has been given power to summon all the birds that fly in midheaven. "Come and gather together for the supper of the great God" (Revelation 19:17 RAV), and they feast on the flesh of the condemned, as they are bidden.

The entire cosmos will be affected when in the end times the angels execute judgment, for their power and authority extend over all creation — the sun, the stars, the waters. An unprecedented judgment will descend, just as the Lord foretold through His prophets, "Behold, the day of the Lord comes, cruel, with wrath and fierce anger, to make the earth a desolation and to destroy its sinners from it...I will make the heavens tremble, and the earth will be shaken out of its place, at the wrath of the Lord of hosts in the day of his fierce anger" (Isaiah 13:9,13).

The intensity of that judgment will be increased when the angels with the bowls of wrath are ordered to bring upon mankind the seven last plagues: foul and evil sores; sea, rivers and springs of water turned into blood; the scorching heat of the sun; total darkness; the drying up of the Euphrates River; and a terrific earthquake. Thus in the age of God's wrath His angels will be employed throughout the universe in carrying out His judgments. They will help to set up the kingdom of God here on earth, and from this we see what an important role the angels play in the completion of God's eternal plans and purposes. Together with Christ the angels will finally rout the army of the Antichrist at the close of the age, displaying as never before their triumphant, victorious might as the holy army of heaven.

Yes, the angels will help to lead the judgments of God to a climax, and thus God's objective will be accomplished. Then all the horrors will fade into the background, and great rejoicing will break out in heaven because the hour of redemption is drawing nigh for the world. When that hour comes, the final outworking of Jesus' sacrifice at Calvary will be demonstrated as Satan is rendered powerless and the new earth comes into being. "Hallelujah! For the Lord our God the Almighty reigns. Let us rejoice and exult and give him the glory" (Revelation 19:6f.). What is true for our personal lives is also true for the earth and mankind: the hour of judgment is the hour of utmost grace. It liberates the world from its bondage to him who led it into ruin by causing sin to reach its zenith.

For the angels too it will be a climactic moment when Satan is taken captive — he who fell away from them and caused such immeasurable heartache. According to the Book of Revelation, the divine judgments executed with the assistance of God's angels before the establishment of the kingdom of God on earth will close with a significant event. An angel will appear with a key and a great chain in his hand, symbolizing the triumphant victory that has been established over the power of Satan and his demons. This is the key to hell, the bottomless pit, into which the angel will throw Satan after first binding him with the chain (Revelation 20:1ff.). And when the thousand years are ended, Satan will be loosed for a little while, only to meet his final doom in the lake of fire (Revelation 20:10).

The victory has been won. Satan is defeated, and the purposes of God have been accomplished with the help of the mighty angels. How glorifying it is for Jesus and the omnipotent God to have such powerful warners, heralds and executors of the divine judgments and counsels — especially in the end times!

9
The Source of Angelic Power

The great power of the holy angels stems from their relationship to God. Their attitude is scarcely comprehensible to us human beings, because our attitude towards God is usually just the reverse. The angels dwell in the presence of God in a constant state of profound reverence and humility. This is what prompts the mighty angelic beings at the throne, the seraphim, to cover their faces when they worship the holy God. As a mark of deepest reverence and submission they cover their feet (Isaiah 6:2). It is as if the angels cannot humble themselves enough before God.

This attitude of the angels towards God is especially remarkable, for they themselves are so glorious. Their power is vast. In their knowledge, ardour and wisdom they reflect the very nature of God, even though they will always remain created beings.

However, the more exalted a being stands in his relationship to God, the greater is his humility. This we can see from Jesus' attitude towards the Father and towards people. Humility is a truly divine attribute. Jesus says, "The Son of man came not to be served but to serve" (Matthew 20:28); "I am among you as one who serves" (Luke 22:27). Of the angels it is written, "Millions of angels were at his service and myriads attended him" (Daniel 7:10 MOFFATT). They stand before the almighty, eternal God, their

Maker, not to rule but ready to serve. This is why it is written in Revelation that they fall prostrate before the throne of God (Revelation 7:11). They always feel constrained to cast themselves down before God. In their humility they cannot bear to stand on the same level as the omnipotent God, although the divine greatness and glory that they reflect should give them far more reason to be proud than us wretched, sinful mortals, who in our arrogance usually dare to stand before God with our heads erect.

Throughout the Bible we are given glimpses of the humble nature of the angels and their readiness to serve. In Hebrews it says that the angels are sent forth to serve the heirs of salvation. The archangel Gabriel introduces himself to Zacharias as a servant. Instead of declaring his power and greatness as a mighty angelic prince, he simply says, "I am Gabriel, who stand [one German Bible translator adds 'as a servant'] in the presence of God, and was sent to speak to you" (Luke 1:19 RAV). Again we are given a glimpse of the humility of the angels. Gabriel emphasizes that he has been sent to Zacharias. He does not bring the message of his own accord, but comes on behalf of someone else: the Lord. He stresses that he is merely a messenger delivering a message from God.

The humility of the angels is also indicated by Jesus' words, "In heaven their angels always behold the face of my Father who is in heaven" (Matthew 18:10). They are completely dependent upon the Father in heaven, and although they are mighty princes they do nothing of their own accord. With their gaze fixed on the countenance of God, they live in total submission to Him, reading in His eyes and hearing from His lips their directives. Minute by minute they look to Him for guidance, and so they always know what they are to do. All their actions are in keeping with His nature, for in their innermost being they have absorbed, as it were, His very features. As Scripture says, they truly are "his servants" and at the same time they are His "mighty ones who do his bidding, who obey his word" (Psalm 103:20f. NIV).

Thus we can well imagine that when they notice an expression of anguished wrath on God's countenance, they immediately carry out His judgments of wrath, as depicted in the Book of Revelation. Or when they see God the Father rejoicing over a penitent sinner, a prodigal son coming home, they too rejoice. Likewise, when they see Jesus radiant with joy at the sight of the bride of the Lamb nearing completion in number and maturity, they may well begin to make preparations for the marriage supper of the Lamb, that great festive occasion.

The angels, with their dependence upon God and their reverent, humble, self-effacing attitude, show forth who God is: their Lord and Maker. Thus they glorify Him before heaven and earth, the entire universe.

The Bible verses about the angels' status as servants bring to mind the words of Michael in the legend mentioned earlier. A voice could be heard, humble but firm: "Who is like God!" And when the Lord asked, "What makes you speak thus?", Michael replied, "Your greatness, Lord, and my nothingness."

Thus the power of the angels and the vastness of their authority stem from their humility and their readiness to serve. In profound reverence the angels lie humbly before God as mere nothings, filled with awe at His omnipotence, holiness and greatness as the Creator God. This is what makes them so great and glorious. They are not concerned about their own glory. They seek nothing for themselves. They live only to glorify God and extol Him. For this reason God has given them such great power and authority, making them princes and mighty ones in His kingdom. Conversely, Lucifer, who sought his own glory and did not want to live in dependence upon God out of love and reverence for Him, lost his glory and his throne.

Michael and all the other angels who humbly acknowledged their nothingness before the omnipotent Creator God became mighty champions and warriors of God, reflecting His glory and receiving great power in order to lead His campaigns to a victorious outcome. This will also become evident in the end times when Michael throws down the dragon (Revelation 12).

From the angels we see that power and authority lie in humility. This is uniquely demonstrated in the life of Jesus. He who was shamefully degraded has been exalted above everything that can be named in heaven and on earth, so that every knee should bow before Him. God has also exalted the angels in their humility — as an example for us.

A further reason for the angels' greatness and authority is their oneness with the will of God. According to Scripture, they are "his servants who do his will...mighty ones who do his bidding, who obey his word" (Psalm 103:21,20 NIV). He who commits himself to the will of God is united with the great and glorious, almighty God who has all things at His disposal and whom nothing can resist.

Who, then, can withstand the one who does everything in union with God, in complete submission to

His will? To be sure, with sinful man this oneness is not possible to the fullest degree. The holy angels, however, live in a state of perfect unity with the will of God. This is why they possess such great power and authority. They do not rebel against God, as we human beings do time and again when with our limited understanding we fail to comprehend the great, omniscient, almighty God and His actions. In their hearts there is no rebellion against His will, no Whys, no questions about His leadings and actions.

The angels are able to submerge their wills completely in the will of God, because they possess the great quality of humility. They declare, "Who is like God!" With all their being they revolve around God, bringing Him honour and worship and seeking no power for themselves. In contrast to the fallen angels, who rose in revolt against God because they could not be like Him, the holy angels are completely one with God and His will. They accept the place assigned to them in God's creative order. Unlike the fallen angels, who work against God, they work solely for God and with Him. Accordingly, God is for them. He is not against them as He is against Satan and the fallen angels, whom He will combat in the final battle and then cast into the lake of fire.

The fact that God is for His holy angels means that He bestows upon them a measure of His infinite power. Unhampered by pride and self-will, which would create a barrier between them and God, the angels can receive freely of the strength, power and ardour in His divine heart. This is what makes them His mighty ones, endowed with divine beauty, power, might and glory. May the angels be a constant incentive for us to be humble like them, living in complete submission to the will of God, so that He can grant us greater power and authority.

10
Angels and Human Beings

Angels and human beings — could there be a greater contrast? Two kinds of beings but worlds apart. We human beings are mortal and bear the imprint of death. The angels are immortal. We human beings are made of flesh and blood and possess earthly bodies. The angels are celestial beings, spirits, not made of flesh and blood. Created as man and woman, we human beings are subject to our human instincts. The angels are sexless (Luke 20:35f.). They have heavenly bodies made of heavenly substance. They are not limited by space and time; they can go through locked doors and yet eat and drink as Jesus did after His resurrection. The angels are not subject to growth or decay, whereas man is. The angels have their abode in heaven, and we on earth. The angels are pure and sinless, whereas we are sinful to the core, born with the taint of original sin. The angels revolve around God, being taken up with Him alone. Every fibre of their being is expressive of reverence and adoration for God. We human beings are still taken up with people and the things of this world — even as believers. We do not revolve around God alone.

Two kinds of beings with completely different, contrasting natures, and two completely different worlds — is this not reason enough to suppose they will be separated for ever? No, according to the eternal decrees of God, angels and human beings, though members of different dimensions of creation, are meant to belong together one day, for as it is written, "You have come to Mount Zion and to the city of the living God, the heavenly Jerusalem, and to innumerable angels in festal gathering, and to the assembly of the first-born...and to the spirits of just men made perfect" (Hebrews 12:22f.). When as overcomers we reach the heavenly goal, we shall not only share the heritage of God's people in the realm of light but also live in the company of the angels. According to Jesus' words, we shall then be like the angels, having no longer an earthly body but a heavenly one. We too shall be spiritual beings, neither marrying nor being given in marriage (Matthew 22:30). Nor shall we be restricted any longer by the laws of space and time.

What tremendous joy Jesus has prepared for us in His kingdom above! There we shall never tire of gazing upon these magnificent angels who with great splendour reflect the image of God, each manifesting another aspect of the divine glory.

Enraptured, we shall listen to the heavenly music of their glorious anthems of worship. We shall speak with them about the mysteries of God and rule with them in His kingdom. In heaven above they will be our brothers. Who can comprehend this? Compared with the pure and sinless angels, the sons of Adam are sinful through and through, characterized by anger, bitterness, impurity, lying and all kinds of wickedness. Some were even servants of Satan, abandoned to sinful ways and sunk below the level of animals.

How can it be that in heaven above we shall be brothers of the angels? This we owe to the outpoured blood of Jesus, His bitter suffering, and His agonizing death on the cross. He saved the ungodly from sin and the power of Satan. He wrought a complete redemption so that prisoners of sin, who placed their faith in Him, were set free from their chains of sin. By pursuing holiness and battling in faith against their sinful nature with its passions and appetites, they overcame powers and principalities inciting them to sin. In this way they were remoulded into the image of God, becoming a "new creation" and "partakers of the divine nature" (2 Corinthians 5:17; 2 Peter 1:4). And in heaven above, having been changed into His likeness, they will reflect His image, just as the angels do in their own way, and so the two will be brothers.

In heaven, the Lamb is worshipped by men and angels alike, though in different ways. Human beings have far greater cause to offer praise and worship, for they have been redeemed by the blood of the Lamb. Their adoration of Jesus, the Lamb that was slain for them, comes from hearts filled with overflowing thanks, fervent love and profound humility because of the wounds their sins inflicted upon Him. The angels worship the Lamb as awed witnesses of the incomprehensible act of God's saving work. They can never fathom the infinite love of the Son, who for the sake of us human beings descended from the throne, leaving behind Him the glory and fellowship of the Father. He abandoned Himself to brutal men, who rejected Him with scorn and mockery, finally torturing and crucifying Him.

Awed by the mystery of such love, the angels will offer praise and adoration for all eternity. Not having personally experienced salvation, they cannot join in the jubilant song of salvation, though they probably yearn to penetrate this mystery (1 Peter 1:12), and in deep reverence they will listen to the anthems of the redeemed in heaven. Thus glorified men and the angels will worship the Triune God, each in his own way, and together they will have a part in His universal rule.

Angels and human beings belong together — but not only later in heaven. Though we are essentially different from the angels, God has appointed them to watch over us in this life as our guardians and warners.

What a privilege for us sinful human beings! Considering the trouble we cause our fellow-men, who find us hard enough to bear although they too are sinners, it is scarcely comprehensible that God should send us His pure and holy angels to guide us on our way. We cause them far more trouble. What sufferings and disappointments they have to undergo on our account! This goes especially for our guardian angel. Truly, we are not worthy of the angels' ministry.

That every person has a guardian angel associated with him in a special way is a token of God's loving care for us. "They [the little ones, which can also be taken to mean the weak and needy] have their guardian angels in heaven, who look continually on the face of my heavenly Father" (Matthew 18:10 NEB). This is how Jesus refers to these angels who are assigned to each of us personally. For the early Christians it was a matter of course that everyone had a guardian angel. Indeed, they even believed that the guardian angel looked like the person in his charge. When the maid Rhoda reported to the believers in Jerusalem that Peter, whom they knew to be in prison, was now standing at the door, they replied, "It is his angel" (Acts 12:15).

108

How wonderful it is that each one of us has his very own angel, who follows the course of his life on earth! What joys and surprises await us in heaven when we shall see him in his glory, power and beauty, and when we thank him and hear how he led us, fought on our behalf, warned us, shed tears for us and rejoiced over us!

Although the angels' primary relationship to us is that of observers and adjudicators, this does not mean that they are impassive critics. On the contrary, they are deeply interested in man's well-being and his conduct towards God throughout his earthly pilgrimage. They follow the destiny of every person, the trials and hardships that come his way, knowing that all the time God in His love seeks to draw each soul to Himself. Their sympathetic concern for us throughout our earthly lives is an indication that the angels are constantly about us. Because we are a "spectacle" to them, as Paul says (1 Corinthians 4:9), we evoke in them either joy or sorrow according to the way we live. If they see us repenting of our sins, turning from paths of wickedness and sinful habits, and following Jesus instead, there is great rejoicing among the angels (Luke 15:10). Conversely, how it must grieve their hearts when we allow Satan to lead us astray, when we become his slaves and yield to sin or when we are hardened in impenitence! Every time we comply with sin, every time we are self-righteous, impenitent and unbelieving, we cause them immeasurable sorrow.

Just as we can bring joy to God the Father, our Lord Jesus and the Holy Spirit when we repent with a humble and contrite heart after every fall, so we can bring joy to the angels, especially our guardian angel. What an effect our behaviour has on the unseen world — be it good or evil!

The angels are not just around each one of us personally but around the whole Body of Christ. Because the angels take such an interest in the Body of Christ, the divine "mystery, which for ages past was kept hidden in God," is to be made known to them, as the apostle Paul writes in his letter to the Ephesians: "His intent was that now, through the church, the manifold wisdom of God should be made known to the rulers and authorities in the heavenly realms" (Ephesians 3:9f. NIV). In 1 Corinthians 11:10 an allusion is made to the angels' interest in the behaviour within the body of believers. For instance, women are bidden to cover their heads "because of the angels". This brings to mind a point made by Paul in 1 Corinthians 4:9, referred to earlier: every person, or in this case the whole body of believers, is being observed by the angels. Nothing escapes their notice. The spiritual condition of the Body of Christ has a corresponding effect upon the angels. They are grieved when there are divisions in the Body of Christ, when believers quarrel and when their lives are dishonouring to the Lord. But when they are "one in heart and mind" and live in reconciliation out of love for Jesus, the angels rejoice.

The apostle Paul was very conscious of the fact that the angels are our spectators. The typical reaction of a keen spectator of a play is that he rejoices or weeps, being caught up in what he sees. Knowing that they were a "spectacle" to the angels, the apostles lived not only in the presence of God but in the awareness of the angelic presence too. In other words, they lived in the company of the angels. The way Paul solemnly charges Timothy in the presence of not only God and Christ Jesus but the holy angels to follow certain instructions implies that one day we

110

shall also have to give account of ourselves before the angels (1 Timothy 5:21).

We heard that the angels will be present on the great and holy occasions when the heavenly court sits in judgment. In the case of the high priest Joshua, an angel pronounced a verdict in his favour when Satan accused him. Coming to Joshua's assistance like an advocate, the angel reprimanded Satan, saying, "The Lord rebuke you, O Satan!...Is not this a brand plucked from the fire?" Then he gave the command to the other angels present: "Remove the filthy garments from him" (Zechariah 3:1-4).

As we have seen, the angels, who are our spectators, also pronounce verdicts upon us, even imposing punishments, as in the case of Zacharias when the angel announced the birth of John the Baptist: "Behold, you will be mute...because you did not believe my words" (Luke 1:20 RAV). Another angel smote Herod "because he did not give glory to God. And he was eaten by worms and died" (Acts 12:23 RAV). Yes, angels execute judgments on people and nations (2 Kings 19:35). The angels, always being on God's side, are opposed to all sin in the life of man. In the account of man's fall we see them standing with flaming sword at the entrance to Eden to guard it from sinful man's pride and disobedience. Since the angels too know all about our deeds, God has given them the authority to inflict punishment. They do so, no doubt, spurred on by the deep reverence they feel for God. At every affront of God they long to use all the power at their disposal to intervene on His behalf and punish those who treat their Lord with disdain.

The angels also have a right to pronounce verdicts, for they have assumed responsibility for our lives. But how painful it must be for the holy angels to judge the wicked and cast them into the terrible kingdom of hell at the end of their earthly lives. How often they must have wept over us when we tolerated the smallest sin in our lives, when we grieved and dishonoured God, whose honour alone they live to magnify.

Minute by minute our whole lives, all our thoughts and actions, be they good or evil, are an open book for God and His angels and for Satan and his demons. Not for a single moment can we hide from their sight. Well aware of this, the apostles were constrained to be "holy in all their conduct". They had not lost that sense of reverence and godly fear as we have largely done today.

All our deeds are registered by God and His angels on the one hand, and by Satan and his demons on the other hand. We are under the observation of both sides — the messengers of light and the messengers of darkness. Either we fill the demons with fiendish delight and the angels with deep grief, or else we make the angels rejoice and the demons scream with fury. For Jesus' sake, who suffered immeasurably to redeem us, let us not grant Satan the triumphant joy of entering the presence of Jesus as our accuser and scornfully declaring what pathetic disciples He has. Instead may we be a joy for God and the angels in all that we say and do.

The fact that with our daily lives we are a "spectacle" to angels and demons alike means that the angels also see when we are in danger. This is why they are constantly battling with the demons on our behalf, our guardian angel no doubt warring especially against the demon commissioned by the prince of hell to lead us into perdition. God has assigned the angels to come to our aid and enter the conflict. The evil spirit, the demon, is not visible to our eyes. But the holy angel can see him. He can ward off the foe and put us on our guard. If angelic princes and demonic principalities battle over the nations in their charge, it stands even more to reason that a guardian angel will battle for the soul entrusted to his care and protection. Luther was aware of this when he wrote: "When I rise in the morning and pray, when I say the morning blessing and go across the field, then I should bear in mind that the angel of God is with me and guarding me well against the devils behind me and before me."

Ever since the angels witnessed that terrible moment when Lucifer turned apostate, they have been entrusted with the important task of fighting against Satan and his demons. The Lord God wages this battle against the demonic forces and the dragon indirectly through Michael, who overthrows the dragon. To His holy and faithful angels God gives the commission to battle against the unfaithful angels.

What a great service the angels do us by engaging in the bitter conflict with the evil spirits and opposing the devil for us! How grateful we should be for their support in our weakness and for their willingness to be God's instruments in the combat with the devil and his hordes. Even we who are sinners and have something of Satan's poison in our fallen natures find it hard to have anything to do with Satan and the demons, who are sinister, vicious and utterly depraved. It costs us a great deal to fight against them when they press us hard or when we battle in faith and prayer for others, who perhaps as a result of dealings with the occult are in bondage to Satan. But the angels are pure, transparent light. They do not know what it is to sin. Can we imagine what this battle must cost them?

Out of love for us and in compliance with God's commands the angels enter warfare with the gruesome, wicked demonic spirits. Because God our Father and our Lord Jesus love us so dearly, They entrust this mission to the angels, who presumably leave their place at the throne repeatedly to enter the battle zone, though always remaining in contact with the throne. What a consolation it is to know: "We are not alone in this struggle. A battle is being fought for us and we need but join forces with the heavenly armies."[15] Yes, "Man has become a battlefield for the angels of God and the devils, but at the same time he is actively involved in this battle."[16]

For our generation, which has entered the endtime era, it is of crucial importance that we reckon with the angels battling against the demons for our sakes, and that we consciously go through life with them. More than any previous generation we shall find ourselves surrounded and harassed by demonic forces. God's chosen ones are the target of Satan and the demons. When they vent their fury on us, it is important that we are aware of the divine power of the angelic princes, the holy angels, who battle for us. Their power is real. Invested with tremendous strength, they are sent forth to minister to the heirs of salvation, that is, God's own.

Yes, these heavenly warriors, who fight on our behalf against the demons, have the power to help us, for they are equipped with the undiminished strength of God. Who can forget the account of the three men in the fiery furnace? "Blessed be the God of Shadrach, Meshach, and Abednego, who has sent his angel and delivered his servants" (Daniel 3:28). The angel of His presence helped His people (Isaiah 63:9), and he will help us. When we come under demonic attack, we who fear the Lord shall be surrounded and assisted by the mighty warriors of God.

Just how real this is can be seen from a testimony from India.[17]

A missionary reported what a native minister told him. As a young man, the minister once met a sorcerer, who praised the power of his spirit and offered to demonstrate it some time. The minister agreed and they fixed a day when they would meet again at the same place. By the power of his evil spirit the sorcerer intended to prevent the minister from coming. It was a duel between spiritual forces. And what happened? At the appointed time the minister appeared, but the sorcerer was nowhere to be seen. The minister then went to the man, who openly admitted, "Well, I sent my spirit to your house to keep you from coming, but he came back to me, saying, 'I can't get through. There are strong men in white standing around the house.'"

Not only are the angels warriors, observers and adjudicators, but they have yet another ministry, a wonderful one that suits their nature. They carry our prayers up to the throne, just as the angel Raphael said to Tobias and his father: "I am Raphael, one of the seven holy angels who present the prayers of the saints and enter into the presence of the glory of the Holy One" (Tobit 12:15). They offer the prayers to God as incense, as John sees in his vision: "Another angel came and stood at the altar with a golden censer; and he was given much incense to mingle with the prayers of all the saints upon the golden altar before the throne" (Revelation 8:3).

And so the angels listen to every single prayer of ours. They rejoice when God receives much adoration, trust and love. With what joy they bring these prayers before God like precious gifts and a sweet-smelling aroma for Him.

The services the angels do us are almost too numerous to be counted. They are always at our disposal, concerning themselves with us.

The angelic ministry of helping, delivering and protecting us is no doubt uppermost in our minds. Considering our helplessness, how often we human beings would have been abandoned to peril and menace, were it not for the help of angels. Martin Luther, who was convinced of the angels' protective care, once said in a sermon: "The good angels are our guards and escorts; they are our servants, appointed to watch over the Christians, so that no harm can befall them. I myself would rather have *one* angel with me than twenty-four Turkish Sultans with all their power and might; and though they might have with them a hundred thousand muskets, all that is nothing in comparison with a single angel."

The Bible reports how Lot was mobbed by the perverted men of Sodom. On his own he would have been overcome by them, for he was outnumbered. But then the angels came to his aid. "They struck with blindness the men who were at the door of the house, both small and great, so that they wearied themselves groping for the door" (Genesis 19:11). Angels saved his life.

Yes, angels step into action when people, cities and countries are faced with a crisis. Such a time of emergency came for Jerusalem when Sennacherib and his mighty army were encamped not far from the city. In deep distress King Hezekiah and the prophet Isaiah cried to the Lord for help, and "The Lord sent an angel who cut down every mighty man of valour,

116

leader, and captain in the camp of the king of Assyria. So he returned shamefaced to his own land" (2 Chronicles 32:21 RAV).

Then there was the time when Peter was enchained in a prison cell. In this distressing situation an angel came and tapped him on the side to wake him up, and the chains fell off his hands (Acts 12:5ff.).

What could we possibly fear seeing that the angels of God, equipped with such divine power, are at our service? Yes, God "will give his angels charge of you to guard you in all your ways". Nor is that all. As we read on, we are given a glimpse of the angels' tender love for us: "On their hands they will bear you up, lest you dash your foot against a stone. You will tread on the lion and the adder, the young lion and the serpent you will trample under foot" (Psalm 91:11-13). Daniel experienced in that terrible and fearful moment when he was cast into the lions' den: "My God sent his angel and shut the lions' mouths, so that they have not hurt me" (Daniel 6:22 RAV).

How comforting is the assurance that when we are assailed, those who are with us outnumber our foes! This is what the prophet Elisha saw when his city was besieged by a great army. He prayed that the eyes of his servant would also be opened to see the angelic hosts surrounding them — mighty warriors, whose power none can withstand (2 Kings 6:14-17).

Faced with the perils of the desert and the menace of hostile tribes, the children of Israel would never have reached the Promised Land if God had not sent them angelic help. "The angel of his presence saved them" (Isaiah 63:9), leading them out of Egypt, through the wilderness, and then on to the Promised Land. Thus Moses testified, "When we cried to the

Lord, he heard our voice, and sent an angel and brought us forth out of Egypt" (Numbers 20:16). Jacob also bore witness to the deliverance he experienced, referring to his angel as "the angel, who has rescued me from all harm" (Genesis 48:16 GNB). A fugitive, exiled from his homeland and in deep distress, he had seen the heavens open and the angels of God ascending and descending on a ladder reaching to heaven (Genesis 28:12).

Angels also minister to believers in their dying hour. Chariots of fire (angels) and horses of fire carried Elijah, that warrior of God, away from this earth (2 Kings 2:11). And for the poor man Lazarus they were the heralds of the recompensing love of the Father carrying him into paradise (Luke 16:22).

It is scarcely comprehensible that the angels should attend to every kind of trouble or need in our lives. Such concern is expressive of great love. Not only do they watch over our souls when they are threatened by Satan, who is bent on leading us into misery, but they take care of us when we are physically in danger. In time of war, in persecution, in every situation when disaster threatens, they are on the spot. When we are faced with a difficult task, they are close beside us to help us make the right decision and see us safely through. Eliezer experienced this when, following Abraham's instructions, he sought a wife for Isaac among Abraham's kindred (Genesis 24:7). The angel led him to the destined woman, whom Eliezer could not have found by himself. And when Elijah, fleeing from Jezebel, was utterly exhausted and almost on the verge of giving up, an angel touched him as he lay there, giving him food and gently advising him, "Arise and eat, else the journey will be too great for you" (1 Kings 19:5-7).

How lovingly the angels watch over those entrusted to them! Just how much they feel for us can be seen from the guardian angel of the city of Jerusalem. The citizens of Jerusalem, who had been in captivity for seventy years, were so much upon his heart that he asked the Lord, "How long wilt thou have no mercy on Jerusalem and the cities of Judah, against which thou hast had indignation these seventy years?" (Zechariah 1:12). Then we read, "The Lord answered gracious and comforting words to the angel." From this we may infer how much the guardian angel must have shared the sorrows of the exiled Jews.

Yes, the angels are very much involved in our earthly lives. As messengers of God they admonish us and give us instructions. They do so as part of their task of guarding and watching over our souls. Luther says in this connection, "God gives guidance through His angels, in that the good angels make their presence felt, either inwardly with a thought or some advice that they put into the mind, or outwardly by giving an indication or placing a difficulty in the way, so that the person is warned and decides to do this or not to do that, to go this way or to avoid going that way, often contrary to his original intentions."

For instance, an angel ordered Elijah to go and meet the messengers of the king, later instructing him not to be afraid but to go with the captain sent by the king (2 Kings 1). With this assurance from the angel he could fearlessly carry out his difficult mission as a prophet of God and tell King Ahaziah the truth.

Likewise, an angel was sent to the God-fearing gentile, Cornelius the centurion, who staring at him in terror, asked, "What is it, lord?" The angel replied, "Send men to Joppa, and send for Simon

119

whose surname is Peter" (Acts 10:3ff. RAV). By following the angel's command, the centurion came to a living faith. And not only that — many gentiles received the gift of the Holy Spirit. This marked a turning-point in the history of the spreading of the Gospel.

Again, an angel of the Lord instructed Peter while in prison, "Wrap your mantle around you and follow me" (Acts 12:7-11). He then led Peter past the guards, through locked doors, and into freedom.

Often the angels give assistance of another kind. With their explanations they help people to understand divine plans and purposes, as in the case of Daniel (Daniel 7:16). To the apostle John an angel showed the City of God and explained to him what must take place (Revelation 21:9ff.; 22:6). Elsewhere in Scripture angels talked with people about the divine happenings in their lives. Only because the angel brought tidings of the new-born Saviour were the shepherds of Bethlehem able to worship the Child in the manger as the Son of God. Similarly, the angels explained to the women at the empty tomb of Jesus that what they were now experiencing was in fulfilment of what Jesus had told them beforehand (Luke 24:4-7).

Yes, the angels are messengers, as signified by the Greek word "angelos", meaning "messenger". They deliver messages to people. Their messages come from God, who is the Truth, whose thoughts are Yea and Amen and who acts upon His word. Thus people who received a message through an angel were never led astray. The demons belong to the kingdom of darkness, deception and lies. The angels are princes in the kingdom of heaven, the kingdom of truth, where all is light and clarity. What they say comes to pass.

120

Although according to human experience and the laws of nature it was impossible for Zacharias and Elizabeth to have a son, the message of the archangel Gabriel came true and a boy was born. When Zacharias responded to the angel's message with unbelief, the angel said he would lose his ability to speak, and so it was. When the archangel Gabriel delivered to Mary the even more incredible message that the Holy Spirit would overshadow her and the holy Child to be born of her would be the Son of God, for with God nothing is impossible, the impossible became a reality. The angel was not telling idle tales. He spoke of actualities, of future events, which then came to pass. This was also Joseph's experience when an angel appeared to him, announcing the birth of Jesus as the Saviour.

The same truth was demonstrated in Abraham's day. Two angels came to Sodom one evening and urged Lot, "Flee for your life" (Genesis 19). The message was not a false alarm or a lie. Lot's life really was at stake, for shortly afterwards the cities of Sodom and Gomorrah were destroyed by the fiery rain of divine judgment. An angel of God also called to Hagar from heaven when she had lost her way in the wilderness. He reassured her, "God has heard the voice of the lad" — and the boy did not die (Genesis 21:17).

An angel of the Lord instructed Philip to go at midday "towards the south along the road which goes down from Jerusalem to Gaza" (Acts 8:26 RAV). And, sure enough, there he met the treasurer of the queen of Ethiopia sitting in his chariot and was able to carry out his important mission.

In the account of how he survived shipwreck, Paul testifies: "There stood by me an angel of the God to whom I belong...and he said, 'Do not be afraid, Paul...lo, God has granted you all those who sail with you'" (Acts 27:23f.) — and so it was.

Angels delivering messages and speaking to us human beings — do we find it hard to understand why that should be? Does God not speak through His Spirit and His prophets, and does Jesus not speak to His disciples through His Spirit? Why, then, should angels also bring us instructions from the Lord? Perhaps we argue: "Shouldn't we just reckon with Jesus helping us? If we also reckon with the assistance of angels, isn't that diminishing the power of Jesus, who alone is our Helper?" Not so. If we say to ourselves, "I'm not going to let anyone but Jesus help me," we actually dishonour Him, for He Himself has sent His angelic hosts to minister to us, and in them He manifests His greatness.

Jesus Himself allowed ministering angels to strengthen Him during His earthly life, especially when attacked by Satan. He availed Himself of their help, though as Son of God He was closest to the Father and could reckon more than anyone else with the direct intervention of the Father. But humility is willing to accept the help of angels. Lowly in heart, Jesus allowed Himself to be strengthened by an angel rather than by the Father during His bitter struggle in Gethsemane (Luke 22:43). The angel, however, was sent by the Father. Indeed, every instance of angelic help should be regarded as a mark of the heavenly Father's love and care and should inspire us to praise Him for it. It is a matter of having the right relationship to God. Then we shall also have the right relationship to the angels.

A comparison can be drawn with our relationship to people. We may express our thanks to them, love and respect them for all the goodness they show us and for the way they assist us. But if our relationship to Jesus is right, He will remain at the centre, as the source of all goodness that we experience through people. We worship Him, and not people. Likewise, we do not worship the angels but God alone.

The same applies to what the holy angels say to us human beings. This does not diminish Jesus' words to us, for they speak to us on behalf of Him. In the Book of Zechariah we read of many conversations that the angel had with Zechariah as he communicated to him the prophetic instructions of God (e.g. Zechariah 1:9; 2:3; 5:5). Perhaps most familiar to us is the conversation in which the angel showed Zechariah a golden lampstand and interpreted the meaning of it at his request (Zechariah 4:1-6).

To be sure, in biblical times angels did not speak to many people, and certainly not to all — and today it is the same. Nonetheless, everyone took it for granted that angels did speak to human beings. In addition to assisting us in our struggles and taking care of us, the angels are commissioned by God to warn and instruct us. In Jesus' time this was evidently a well-known fact, judging from the reaction of some of the people when they heard the Father speaking from heaven in answer to Jesus' prayer. Not knowing whose voice it was, they commented, "An angel has spoken to him" (John 12:29). Likewise, when Paul was called to account before the Sanhedrin, after publicly relating the story of his conversion, some of the scribes argued, "What if a spirit or an angel spoke to him?" (Acts 23:9).

In other words, it is not only God who speaks to people. Angels also communicate with them. Admittedly, false claims have been made about visions and voices of angels. Or misconceptions have arisen because the existence of angels was overemphasized and Christ was no longer the centre of a person's spiritual life. Such was the case in the church at Colossae. With a false notion of humility people sought to imitate the supernatural nature of the angels and to attain it by legalistic mortification of the flesh (Colossians 2:18ff.). But misconceptions and misuse of a thing do not make it wrong in itself. The fact remains that in addition to their ministry of adoration the angels are sent forth to serve us human beings that we might inherit salvation. As living beings they communicate with us and act in our lives.

Today, as in biblical times, only a few people have been granted the privilege of having an angel appear to them and speak with them. But even if we do not usually see the angels with our eyes or hear their voices with our ears, for the unseen world seldom lifts its veil, they do speak to us in our hearts. Just as we have, no doubt, heard the deceptive voices of Satan and the evil spirits in our hearts without actually hearing them acoustically, we may assume that the holy angels of God speak in our hearts and stir our consciences as ambassadors of God and messengers of light. When we are inwardly convicted or admonished or when we feel drawn to God and His commandments, could this not sometimes be the work of our angel? And have we ever found ourselves breaking something or bumping into something, for example, after speaking an unkind word or thinking an unloving thought? Might this not also be our angel warning and rebuking us?

Because the angels have the task of admonishing us, the Lord says, "Attend to him [the angel], listen to what he says; never defy him...since I am manifest in him" (Exodus 23:21 MOFFATT). God thus warns Moses, saying that otherwise the angel will not pardon him. In the lives of Zacharias and Joshua we have already seen that angels have the authority to punish and pardon. An analogy from everyday life may help us to understand this. After deliberately disobeying someone in authority, do we not ask his forgiveness? But even if he pardons us, the fact remains that God alone can grant us remission of sins.

The angel is like an extension of the arm of God, a vessel of His authority. The fact that God commands us to heed the angels is a proof that the angels, endowed with superior mental power, ability and authority, have a higher rank than man (cf. 2 Peter 2:11).

Behind the activity of the angels we need to see the immeasurable love of God in sending His angels to help us. For it is not only the Father, the Son and the Holy Spirit who love us, teach us, admonish us, warn and rebuke us, so that we might inherit salvation, but as we sing in a seventeenth-century Easter hymn, "God and the angels love us." What a wonderful array of heavenly aid for us sinful human beings!

Truly, every provision has been made for us to reach the heavenly goal: Jesus intercedes for us at the throne; the Holy Spirit admonishes us; the angels battle for our sakes. If we do not reach the goal, even though we believed in Jesus' act of salvation, the angels will testify to the love, the pains and efforts spent on us — and that will speak against us, though no doubt our guardian angel will plead for us to the very end. Do we realize what it means to be not only in the hands of the living God but in the hands of His angels, to be dependent upon their verdict, their efforts on our behalf, and their assistance?

Do our hearts not rejoice and give thanks at the thought that God and His angels love us dearly and take care of us? If we are filled with gratitude towards people for coming to our rescue when we are in distress, how much more grateful should we feel towards our guardian angel for all his services! If here on earth we have the desire to thank another person, a sinful human being like us, for suffering on our behalf and helping us, how much more should this be so in our relationship to the angels, who take great pains over us in this life, never tiring in their assiduous attention of us!

11
Instances of Angelic Help
Experienced Today

The protection, help and wonderful deliverance experienced as a direct result of angelic intervention are not restricted to remote biblical times; they are also evident today. Jesus Christ is the same yesterday and today, and so too are His angels, for they belong to Him. May the following examples serve to illustrate this.

A little boy carelessly strayed from the sidewalk on to the street, where he was immediately run over by a truck. A number of people, including a nurse, saw the accident, which occurred within seconds. Contrary to the expectations of the eye-witnesses, the boy got up from under the vehicle and went his way, only slightly scratched and covered with dust.

Humanly speaking, it was an impossibility! The nurse rushed towards him, exclaiming, "You must have had a good angel!", whereupon he replied with all the simplicity and candour of a child, "No, there were two of them!" In the moment of peril the boy must have had a glimpse beyond the veil. Who can doubt such a convincing answer?[18]

A kindergarten teacher recalls a similar occurrence:

A child that had been run over by a car should

really have been killed or seriously hurt. But it did no more than frighten him. He said to the teacher, "Didn't you see him [the angel] lift the wheel?"

In 1953 a church newspaper in Augsburg, Bavaria, reported the following incident:

During the month of September, round about Michaelmas Day [the festival celebrated in honour of the archangel Michael], a showcase displayed a picture of an angel protecting a child on a busy city street. Filled with interest, some children stood in front of the window to look at the picture. Among them was the child of an atheist. The other children laughed because she did not understand the meaning and so a neighbour's child, a little girl, explained what a guardian angel was.

A week later the atheist came to the girl's father greatly upset. "Once and for all, I will not have your girl putting silly ideas into the head of my child. I won't stand for it! My child doesn't need any guardian angel!"

Later that evening, on his way home, the atheist was annoyed to see the picture still on display in the showcase. Then he came to the crossing where the traffic lights were. Red — yellow — green. Now it was safe to cross. A useful device! What did one need a guardian angel for?

Across the heavy stream of traffic a high-pitched voice reached his ears: "Daddy, yoo-hoo, Daddy!" There was his little daughter waving to him from the window in the fourth storey of their apartment building. He raised his hand to wave back. Soon he would be with her. But what was she doing? She was standing on the windowsill and leaning forward as if she wanted to come to him.

He let out a cry, which even brought the busy traffic to a standstill, and, reeling backwards, he covered his eyes. From the window high up in the apartment building his child tumbled to the ground. Without doubt, she would be dashed to pieces.

Then he felt a hand on his shoulder. It was his neighbour. "But look, she's alive!" The man raised his head. Was he seeing an apparition in broad daylight? Still dazed from the fall, but apart from that virtually unharmed, the child got up from the pavement. The awning of a grocer's shop had acted as an interceptor, lessening the impact of the fall.

The little girl had had a scare but that was about all. She rushed to her father, who shook his head in disbelief. "I really do have a guardian angel!" she said. "Didn't you see him? I did, Daddy. He was like a bright shining light and he carried me!"[19]

From the mission field came the report:

A Christian experienced what was clearly an act of divine intervention when his little girl fell into a mill-race and drifted towards the mill wheel while the mill was in action. Horrified, he rushed to the channel only to find his little one standing on the bank, dripping wet. "A big brother in white clothes pulled me out," she said. God had sent an angel.[20]

The experience of Hedinger (1664-1704), a court chaplain in southern Germany, lies further back in time, but it too bears witness to the reality of angelic activity.

With his candid remarks about Duke Eberhard Ludwig's immoral life Hedinger once infuriated the duke to such an extent that he was summoned to the duke's private quarters, where the latter intended to lay violent hands on him.

When he appeared, the duke barked at him, "Why didn't you come on your own, as I ordered you?"

"Your Highness, I have come on my own," Hedinger replied.

"But you are not alone," the duke insisted and kept staring in horror to the right of Hedinger.

At that the latter replied, "I have truly come on my own, Your Highness. But should it have pleased the almighty God to place an angel at my side in this hour, I know nothing of this."

Visibly distraught, the duke dismissed him with a wave of the hand.[21]

Wonderful instances of angelic help in times of deadly peril were experienced by the well-known man of God, Sadhu Sundar Singh of India.

During one of his itineraries in Tibet he was condemned to death. With a broken arm he spent three agonizing days and nights in a murky, disused well, in the midst of a decaying mass of putrid bodies of criminals condemned before him. In prayer he prepared himself for death and as he did so he was wonderfully comforted and cheered by the sense of his Saviour's presence in that nauseous pit.

On the third night the iron door sealing the top of the well was opened and a voice instructed him to grasp the rope that would be let down to him. With his good arm he took hold of the rope, was pulled out and so rescued. In addition, his battered arm was healed by the hand of his mysterious helper, who then immediately disappeared. After a few days' rest Sundar Singh began preaching again. When he was led before his judge, the lama, the latter was horrified to find attached to his own belt the only key to the well. He thought it had been stolen. Sundar Singh himself shared this with with me [the writer of this report], and like him I could not help thinking it was an angel that had delivered him.[22]

On another occasion when he was in Tibet, Sundar Singh had a similar experience.

In vain he had tried to find open doors for his message in a village; the people refused to hear him, and because of their hostile attitude he was finally forced to retire to a mountain cave. In the evening the villagers, armed with clubs and stones, made their way to his hide-out, intending to kill him. Then all of a sudden they drew back in alarm and called from a distance, "Tell us, who is that man in the shining garment standing beside you, and who are all those others surrounding you?" Sundar Singh replied that he was on his own, but the people were insistent...Angels of God had saved his life.[23]

Round about the year 1860 a missionary couple of the United Evangelical Mission serving among the Bataks in Sumatra also experienced how God allowed the angels to assume visible form when protecting them.

Their predecessors, two American missionaries, had been killed and eaten by the sav-

131

ages. The husband reported that in the beginning he was often overcome with an indescribable fear at night and would rise and pray with his wife for a long time. One day a Batak came to him and asked him to show him the guards whom he had placed around his house.at night. In vain the missionary assured him that he had no guards. The Batak refused to believe him and asked if he could search the whole house. But he found nothing.

Then he related that they had decided to kill the missionary and his wife. Yet when they arrived at his house at night, they found two rows of guards standing there with shining weapons. They hired a killer, who, calling them cowards, declared that he would force his way through these guards. But he too returned, saying, "No, I didn't dare. A double row of men were standing there with their weapons blazing like fire!" Finally, they gave up trying to kill the missionary and his wife.

When the tribesman expressed astonishment that the missionary himself had not seen the guards, the missionary was able to witness to him, saying, "Look, this book is the Word of our great God and in it He promises to protect us. We firmly believe this Word and so we don't need to see the guards. But you don't believe in Him and therefore the great God has to show you these guards in order that you will learn to believe."[24]

A moving testimony of some thirty years ago comes from a preacher in southern Germany.

It was a winter day and dusk was falling. The last stretch of the way to the village led through a big forest. There wasn't a soul in sight and yet the nearer I came to the woods, the heavier my heart grew. I would repeatedly sigh, "O Lord, be merciful to me." The moment I entered the woods, I felt surprisingly calm and at peace. It was as if someone were walking beside me, his arm frequently brushing against my sleeve. But I saw and heard no one...At last the woods lay behind me, and I safely reached the first houses with their lit-up windows. The feeling that someone was accompanying me was gone.

That night I had a frightening dream. I saw myself lying on the ground, battered to death. A voice said, "That's what you would look like now if I hadn't protected you!"...Three months later I found out that on that winter evening a number of youths...had lain in ambush for me at the edge of the forest. It was their firm intention to kill me. They hated me because through the influence of my Bible classes a number of their girl friends no longer wanted to go with them to dances and parties. After they had returned, the youths told their companions that they saw me coming on my own when all of a sudden a tall man appeared at my right-hand side and walked with me till the end of the woods. They didn't see him come or go, and he vanished as mysteriously as he had appeared.

Here was the explanation for that inexplicable and puzzling experience I had had. My life was in grave danger and one of His "ministering spirits" was sent to protect me in a wonderful way![25]

Yes, in this day and age we especially have cause to be thankful for the wonderful help of angels. We have entered the last times. The earth has become a battlefield for the demons, who not only seek to lead us astray but are bent on destroying everything, our health, our bodies, our very existence. An alarm signal is thus sounding for the angelic world. When a person or nation is in extreme danger, the moment has come for the angels to step into action and bring help and deliverance. Now when hordes of demons are swarming across the earth and attacking mankind, we can count on God sending more angels than ever from His heavenly world. He equips them with a double portion of power, for in these end times Satan and his demons are violent and angry, seeking to extend their influence to the greatest possible degree.

A colossal battle has broken out, and without the help of the angels we shall not be able to come through victoriously. Whom do they assist? We may assume that everyone has a guardian angel, for the angels take an interest in every single person, anxious that one and all should receive help in body and soul. However, if a person abandons himself to sin and Satan — as will often be the case in the end times — he can restrain his guardian angel, for man always has freedom of will.

One thing is clear: the angels especially take care of those who fear God. "The angel of the Lord encamps all around those who fear him, and delivers them" (Psalm 34:7 RAV). Thus a man like Daniel received a great deal of angelic help in the way of instruction and deliverance. It is significant that the Bible describes him as being a God-fearing man with a contrite heart. Thus it is not by chance that the angel Gabriel, coming to him "in swift flight", said, "At the beginning of your supplications a word went forth, and I have come to tell it to you, for you are greatly beloved" (Daniel 9:23). What kind of prayer was this? We read that Daniel sought the Lord by prayer and supplications with fasting and sackcloth and ashes. He humbled himself, confessing his own sins and the sins of his people.

Angels are holy beings, and their help does not come automatically. Just as we can forfeit God's help through disobedience, pride and other sins, forcing God to set Himself against us, so we can also forfeit the help of our guardian angel.

For the end-time generation it is of utmost significance that those who walk in the way of the Lord by faith in Jesus Christ are under the special care of the angels. Does not Holy Scripture clearly teach that the angels are "sent forth to minister for those who will inherit salvation" (Hebrews 1:14 RAV), that is, particularly for the believers? In view of the end times, the time of great affliction, the Lord assures them that He "knows how to deliver the godly out of temptations" (2 Peter 2:9 RAV), just as He delivered Lot long ago. Amid the hardships of the end times, amid the perils of war, revolution and persecution, the God-fearing will experience countless instances of miraculous deliverance and protection as others have experienced before them in times of war and chaos.

The following is the testimony of a young woman who was later to become a Sister of Mary. Towards the end of World War II, before the foundation of our Sisterhood, she was serving as an infants' nurse in Danzig. However, with the advance of the Russian army, she was forced to flee with the children in her care. This is her account of what happened when the troops eventually caught up with them:

At two o'clock in the morning there were loud noises out in the corridor. "They've come!" I said to myself. I wanted to dash to the older children, so that they wouldn't be afraid. But the Russians were already there, and all I could do was to withdraw into the bathroom to get away from the corridor. There I busied myself with the laundry, which had been soaking. Then a soldier came in, shut the door behind him and locked it. He gesticulated and spoke, fiddling with the buckle of his belt. Understanding that he wanted to take a bath, I quickly emptied the bathtub and pointed to the soap and towel. He grew angry, pulled out his revolver and pointed it at me. I was terrified that he was going to shoot me.

At that moment I felt someone take my right hand and lead me past the Russian and out into the corridor. I did not touch the door handle or unlock the door, for I was petrified with fear.

In the hallway many Russians were standing with our Ukrainian ward maid. They were laughing together and one of them yanked off my nurse's cap. Half-dazed, I went into the infants' room and placed myself between two cots, but the Russian soldier followed me. He stood before me, a couple of yards away, looking steadily at me, but saying and doing nothing. After a few minutes he turned and left.

During those April days in 1945, after we were overrun by Russian troops for the second time, the women in our area suffered immeasurably. The nights were filled with cries of terror. Together with our children, who had been gathered from various hospitals, we had found a temporary lodging in a small makeshift kindergarten. Since some of the infants had been born prematurely, it was necessary to work at night — though owing to lack of electricity our light came from stubs of candles. As the only house in the entire place with lights on, we were exposed to great danger. Yet people called it "the island of peace". Consequently, the stream of women and girls seeking refuge grew from night to night — and so too the danger.

One day a lady came with her girl and boy, who must have been about eight and twelve years old, and begged us to take the children, since she couldn't possibly spend another one of those nights with them. With heavy hearts we took the children, not knowing whether they would ever be united with their mother again.

The two children, who had a totally unchristian upbringing, had never seen anyone pray. That evening as we prayed with the older children, the new boy instead of folding his hands stared into the distance with wide open eyes. We sang, "...That we in safety now may rest, angelic hosts the Lord does send, placing their golden weapons around our bed." When we said Amen, the boy came up to me spontaneously and drew me out of the building into the open air. He kept tapping his breastbone and said, "Up to here. It came up to here on them." I asked him what he meant. Then, pointing to the gutter on the roof of the building, he repeated, "The gutter came up to here on them!" I asked further, "Who are you talking about?" Then he told me that on every corner of the building he saw a man all ablaze — and these men were so tall that they towered above the roof. Now it was clear to me why this house could be called "the island of peace".

If the angels help those who fear the Lord, as Holy Scripture says, then what a challenge that is for us! We who have been born into this day and age are summoned to live as truly God-fearing souls. In contrast to the licentiousness of our times we are challenged to take the commandments of God all the more seriously and abide by them. It is vital that with all our might we resist the deceptions of Satan, whether it be in the realm of permissiveness, anti-authoritarianism or humanism, or whether it be in the realm of hypocrisy, fault-finding or irreconciliation. God will rescue only the God-fearing out of the hour of trial, which is coming on the whole world. Indeed, when the Lord comes again from heaven with His angels, the God-fearing will be caught up to be with Him (2 Thessalonians 1:7; 1 Thessalonians 4:16f.). When we reach this goal, the angels, including our guardian angel, will probably be there to receive us and we shall thank them. Then we shall dwell with the angels in the City of God, filled with awe and wonder that God should grant us sinners this privilege. May we learn to live in their company here and now, as St. Augustine said:

> Transferred into the kingdom of Jesus Christ,
> we have already drawn closer to the angels.
> The kingdom of God on earth
> and the kingdom of heaven
> belong to both of us,
> and so let us live in
> the company of the angels
> here and now.

To this we could add: And one day above we shall unite with them in glorifying God, who out of the abundance of His goodness and great love has placed His holy angels, His celestial armies, at our side.

138

Notes

1 Cf. Friso Melzer, *Die Christusbotschaft in Indien* (Stuttgart: Kreuz Verlag, 1948).
2 Kurt E. Koch, *Seelsorge und Okkultismus* (Wüstenrot: Kurt Reither Verlag, 1953), pp.135f.
3 *Ibid.*, pp.155f.
4 Cf. Gerhard Jan Rötting, *Rot oder tot* (Gnadenthal: Präsenz Verlag, n.d.).
5 Otto Riecker, ed., *Ruf aus Indonesien* (Lahr-Dinglingen: Verlag der St. Johannis Druckerei, 1971), pp.44ff.
6 Basilea Schlink, *Songs and Prayers of Victory* (Darmstadt: Evangelical Sisterhood of Mary, 1978), pp.30,29.
7 Basilea Schlink, *Praying Our Way Through Life*, 3rd ed. (London: Marshall, Morgan & Scott, 1975), pp.31f.
8 Cf. E. Schick, *Vom Dienst der Engel* (Basel: Verlag Heinrich Majer, 1940).
9 F. Bettex and D. Haarbeck in F. Heitmüller, *Engel und Dämonen, eine Bibelstudie* (Hamburg: Reich & Heidreich, Evgl. Verlag, 1948).
10 Hans Kühn, *Reich des lebendigen Lichts – die Engel in Lehre und Leben der Christenheit* (Berlin: Oswald Arnold Verlag, n.d.).
11 Hermann Leitz, *Die Engel, ihr Wesen und Werk*, 4th ed. *Engel gibt es* (Leipzig and Siegen: Wilh. Schneider Verlag, 1948 and 1969), p.54.
12 *Ibid.*, p.55.
13 Kühn, *op.cit.*

14 Cf. A.C. Gaebelein, *Die Welt der Engel* (Huttwil: Verlag Müller-Kersting, 1932), pp.6f.
15 Magdalene Vedder, Hans Urner and Hildegard Jaecks, eds., *Vom Dienst der Engel* (Berlin: Evang. Verlagsanstalt, 1952), p.7.
16 Ruth Führer, *Von den Engeln* (Gladbeck: Schriftenmissions Verlag, 1957), p.10.
17 Cf. Melzer, *op.cit.*
18 Wilhelm Horkel, *Botschaft von drüben* (München: Neubau Verlag, 1949), p.63.
19 Cf. A.M. Weigl, *In Gottes Vaterhand* (Altötting: Verlag St. Grignionhaus, 1971), pp.77ff.
20 *Mitteilungen* der Liebenzeller Mission in Leitz, *op.cit.*, p.73.
21 Fr. Baun in Leitz, *op.cit.*, p.76.
22 Bauer in Leitz, *op.cit.*, pp.74f.
Cf. Max Schaerer, *Sadhu Sundar Singh, ein Apostel in Indien* (Gütersloh: Verlag C. Bertelsmann, 1922), pp.64ff.
23 H. Großmann in Leitz, *op.cit.*, p.75.
24 Cf. Richard Schmitz, *Engeldienste* (Witten: Bundesverlag, 1963), pp.32f.
25 Johannes Blum in Leitz, *op.cit.*, p.77.

Other books by Basilea Schlink
for your further interest

WHAT COMES AFTER DEATH? –
THE REALITY OF HEAVEN AND HELL
126 pp.

One thought of heaven makes us forget all earthly sorrow. But this is true only when we have a very real concept of heaven. This book seeks to paint a vivid picture of the world above. But equally realistic is the description of hell and the Biblical answer to one of today's most pertinent questions, "What comes after death?"

PATMOS –
WHEN THE HEAVENS OPENED   128 pp.

Vividly and arrestingly Basilea Schlink takes us into the events of the mighty revelation once given on the island of Patmos. Today they are beginning to be fulfilled before our very eyes. This timely book helps us to see the age we are living in and will be a source of encouragement to us in these dark days. It gives our generation a completely new perspective to the future and creates in us a tremendous hope.

HIDDEN IN HIS HANDS   96 pp.

An encouraging selection of spiritual devotions. As we read this book, we shall discover how to experience security in God, and this will return to us as a source of strength and comfort in times of hardship.

THE CHRISTIAN'S VICTORY 192 pp.
(American title: YOU WILL NEVER BE THE SAME)

How can we overcome sin? Asked this question, Basilea Schlink set about prescribing "spiritual medicine", dealing one by one with the sinful traits which mar the Christian's life, helping us to recognize them in ourselves, and pointing out the remedy. We *can* be transformed by gaining victory over our sins in the power of Jesus Christ, our risen Lord and Saviour.

RULED BY THE SPIRIT 132 pp.

As in the days of the early Church, described in the Book of Acts, the power of God to guide and inspire individuals who dedicate their lives wholly to Him is still operative today; this is the kernel of Basilea Schlink's challenging message in this book.

REPENTANCE – THE JOY-FILLED LIFE 96 pp.

Repentance – a golden key that opens the door to a joy-filled life. It has power to transform hearts and situations.

THOSE WHO LOVE HIM 96 pp.

There is a very great difference between someone who is a Christian every day and an "everyday Christian". This book is a real help and counsel against all the deadly nominal and lukewarm Christianity that is always with us…it is a book for those who are looking for good counsel on total and decisive discipleship. It shows clearly, practically and with urgency the way of yielded and unselfish love for Jesus.

THE HIDDEN TREASURE IN SUFFERING
96 pp.

Cares — Strained Relationships — Fear — Illness — Weariness — Loneliness — Inner Conflict — Personality Problems — Unanswered Prayers — Untalented — Growing Old — Want and Need — Fear of Death — Unfair Treatment — Facing Hatred and Slander...

From the wealth of her personal experience Mother Basilea Schlink shares how we can find the treasure that lies hidden in every trial and hardship.